CONFRONTATION
for Better or Worse!

by Bernard G. Berenson
and Kevin M. Mitchell

CONFRONTATION!
For better or worse
Bernard G. Berenson
Center for Human Relations and Community Affairs
American International College

and

Kevin M. Mitchell
Department of Psychology
Athens, Georgia

Human Resource Development Press, Inc.
Box 222, Amherst, Massachusetts, 01002

HRD PERSPECTIVE SERIES

Under the Editorial Direction of
Robert R. Carkhuff
Carkhuff Associates, Inc.
Developers of Human Technology
Box 228, Amherst, Massachusetts 01002
Box 50178, 1 Main Place, Dallas Texas 75250

To
Our Wives
Gloria and Rosamond
Love

Table of Contents
Confrontation! For Better or Worse · · ·

Our early work in helping and human relationships led us to the recognition that being responsive to the helpee's experience is insufficient in and of itself to effect maximum benefits for the helpee. Concisely, understanding is not enough! Effective helpers must also be able to help the helpees to do something about what they understand. In order to help the helpee to do something, the helpers must do something themselves. In the context of understanding, they must initiate from their own experience. Indeed, there is no responsiveness without initiative — no understanding without action. This learning led us to investigate the effects of helper initiative dimensions — among them, confrontation.

Dr. Berenson's and Dr. Mitchell's work is the latest work on confrontation. To be sure, it is the most comprehensive treatment of initiative dimensions. Its research underpinnings, *Chapters 2, 3 and 4,* are creative and solid, the designs simplified by an experienced hand, the statistical analyses appropriately sensitive to the criteria of rigor and meaning.

Its rich, clinical learnings, *Chapters 1, 5 and 6,* are vast. There is a breadth and depth previously unknown on this initiative dimension. This work will serve as a classic from which scholars in the area will draw in decades to come.

It is a masterpiece of human understanding: of pathology seen through the eyes of health; written in a crusty, confronting style dictated by perceptive — no, penetrative and incisive — eyes that see to the soul of man in all of his humanity and inhumanity.

Berenson's most significant contribution is his perspective. Confrontation is never **necessary** and never **sufficient**; but, in the hands of those few who have the skills and, thus, the right to help, confrontation may be an efficient means to personal growth and development.

Berenson views discrepancies in the experience of the helping relationship as the central impediment to helpee growth. For him, confrontation is an active, evaluative, subjective response which offers the helpee much-needed feedback about his impact upon the helper. In the hands of an effective person, then, confrontation may be a lever to more significant helping involvement on the part of the helper.

That confrontation is inherent to helping is implied. Indeed, confrontation is inherent to all human interactions other than those between two or more fully functioning persons. The very nature of a meeting between sickness and health implies confrontation. To be sure, confrontation is inherent to all relationships involving sickness. And it is sickness that issues the challenge because health has made itself available and, thus, seemingly vulnerable.

Berenson suggests that the helpee views himself as a consequence of his distortions of others. Extended, this means that he also views his sick self as a consequence of others' distortions of him. In other words, the helpee is saying, "I'm no more or less sick than anyone else." Shunning responsibility, he adds, "It's the other people's sickness that made me this way." In effect, his very presence in helping confronts the helper's health: "If I can get away with my sickness with you, I am less sick than you." The helpee's challenge is a bold one indeed: "I come to helping not to be changed but to reaffirm my sickness — if I can get away with it with you, I can get away with it with anyone." Effective helping is a process where the helper sticks the helpee with his health. Ineffective helping is a process where each jockeys to stick the other with his pathology.

Berenson sees confrontation in dimensions that converge with human experience. Experiential confrontations are defined as therapist-initiated responses to discrepancies between the helper's experience of the helpee and the helpee's expression of his experience of himself. Didactic confrontations involve the helper's direct clarification of the helpee's misinformation or information about relatively objective aspects of the world or the helping relationship. Confrontations of "strength" refer to the experiential confrontations which focus upon the helpee's resources and confrontations of "weakness" refer to experiential confrontations which focus on the helpee's liabilities of pathology. Finally, confrontations involving "Encouragement to Action" emphasize the helper's pressing the helpee to act upon his world in some reasonable, appropriate and constructive manner, and discouraging a passive stance toward life. These dimensions of confrontation add a wealth of knowledge to our understanding of the ingredients of helping effectiveness.

Most important, high and low functioning therapists confront their helpees differently. First, those helpers who demonstrated low levels of responsive skills also demonstrated low levels of intiative skills. In turn, those helpers who exhibited a high level of responsive skills, also demonstrated a high level of initiative skills. Second, the high level helpers employed significantly more experiential confrontations than did the low level helpers. Where low level helpers confronted, they were more likely to confront with weakness than strength. Third, high level helpers offered an increasing number of experiential confrontations over time. As they came to know more about their helpees, they pressed to become still more involved with them. Fourth, high level helpers also employ more didactic confrontations than their low functioning counterparts. However, the didactic confrontations appear to be less and less important to helpee development over the course of helping. Finally, high level helpers use many times more confrontations of strength than low level helpers. Similarly, the latter use many times more confrontations of weakness than the effective helpers. These findings are consistent with previous research on helping effectiveness. Their implications for growth and development are profound.

Helpers who are fully functioning on both responsive and initiative dimensions can serve as both model and agent for the helpee's development. With time and human contact, they will move in the direction of the helper's functioning. They will grow — physically, emotionally and intellectually.

Conversely, the helpees of helpers who are less than fully functioning on the responsive and initiative dimensions are doomed. With time and contact, they can only deteriorate as a consequence of another of a never-ending series of relationships that promised hope but delivered only failure. They will die — first emotionally, then intellectually, finally physically.

The implications are direct — life or death for the helpee — promised and delivered by helpers who are alive — or dead. There is nothing more — or less!

Finally, there are model-building implications to this important work. If we view the model for effective helping as involving helpee exploration, understanding and action, then the time and place of effective confrontations are detailed. The outcome of effective helping

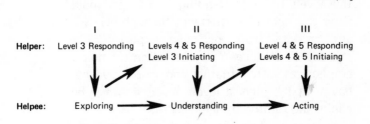

Figure 1: Helper and helpee behaviors in phases of helping

is some tangible change or gain in the helpee's behavior. In order to demonstrate such change or gain, the helpee must act. In order to act, the helpee must have some idea of where he is and where he is going. The helpee must understand himself. In order to understand himself, the helpee must have some idea of where he is "coming from". The helpee must explore himself. Exploring where he is. Understanding where he is in relation to where he wants to be. Acting upon how to get from where he is to where he wants to be. Exploration! Understanding! Action! These are the conditions of helping. These are the conditions of learning. These are the conditions of living.

Certain helper behaviors elicit these process indices of helping effectiveness. When the helper is responsive to the helpee's experience at levels that the helpee is expressing himself, *interchangeable responsiveness — level 3 on 5-point scales,* then the helper elicits and reinforces helpee self-exploration. When the helper is responsive to the helpee at levels beyond where the helpee has expressed himself, *additive understanding — levels 4 and 5,* then the helper elicits and reinforces helpee self-understanding. In order to move to additive levels of understanding, the helper must filter the helpee's experience through his own and initiate from his own experience at minimal levels, *level 3.* Lastly, when the helper emphasizes both initiative and responsive behavior at the highest levels, *levels 4 and 5,* he elicits and reinforces helpee action.

Now it is clear that helper confrontations are least appropriate during the helpee exploration phase when the helper is trying to get to know the helpee's experience. It is also clear that helper confrontations, if any, are most appropriate during the helpee action phase when the helper is trying to facilitate the helpee's development of constructive behavior. There is a place for confrontation to be introduced but not emphasized at the highest levels of initiative during the understanding phases of helping. Accordingly, Berenson has assigned confrontation its proper place.

In order to understand his perspective, the reader must understand that each phase of helping is a microcosm of the other phases. Within each of the phases — indeed, within each helping contact — exploration, understanding and action occur.

Berenson establishes a sequence of confrontations and sets them for the most part in the third phase of helping, the action phase. He establishes three phases of confrontation within the third phase of helping. The effective helper first emphasizes experiential and didactic confrontations which lead within the action phase of helping to increased helpee self-exploration. The effective helper next offers confrontations of strength and weakness as each is appropriate in order to facilitate improved self-understanding by the helpee of his resources. Finally, the effective helper stresses encouragement to action confrontations that lead to action behavior on the part of the helpee. The training implications of this model are critical for they suggest the responses and the context within which confrontations may be effective — if they need to be employed.

In an age when everybody is confronting everyone else, and many are making a good living off either confronting or being confronted, this book puts confrontation in perspective. It assigns confrontation its proper role and function — a very small place, if any, and then only when the appropriate people and conditions are present. When the confronters and the consenters realize that there is nothing for which either may aspire, then the gods of gimmicks, the avoiders of love and responsibility, come tumbling down. "But what will I replace my gimmicks with?", they ask. "Hard work and an expanded response repertoire", Berenson answers.

In summary, this is a book of major consequence to a profession, a people and an age. It has been a privilege for me to be associated with this man and his work. I

cannot pay greater personal tribute than the
creativity that this book has stimulated in
me — a sampling of which I have presented
herewith. I believe this work must be read by
all of those concerned with human effectiveness in our time.

Robert R. Carkhuff, PhD.
Amherst, Massachusetts
January, 1974.

Dr. Bernard G. Berenson is Chairman, Department of Human Relations and Professor of Psychology and Education, American International College, Springfield, Massachusetts. He was formerly director of clinical training programs in Counseling Centers at the state universities of New York, Maryland and Massachusetts. Dr. Berenson is co-author of ''Beyond Counseling and Therapy and "Sources of Gain in Counseling and Psychotherapy," two of the most widely adopted textbooks in counseling and clinical training programs.

Dr. Kevin M. Mitchell is Director of the Psychology Clinic, and Associate Professor of Psychology, University of Georgia, Athens, Georgia. He was formerly Research Associate, Arkansas Research and Rehabilitation Center, University of Arkansas. He has published widely in psychological, educational and rehabilitation journals.

We have written this book in response to the wide variety of uses and abuses of confrontation. It is our contention that confrontation can be for better or for worse. The conditions for its constructive use must be made explicit. Beyond this, we have found that confrontation can take many forms.

In addition, confrontation must be put into a broad and systematic context of helping. We have attempted to develop such a perspective out of a blend of our research and experience.

Our efforts culminated in a model for practice and research. In a larger sense, this work and the implications of our observations have direct ties to a growing technology of human resource development operationalized by Robert R. Carkhuff. With this technology, confrontation may be efficient but not necessary or sufficient.

In addition to the model for research and practice, we have listed the facilitative uses of confrontation. We detail the kinds of confrontation as well as how they are used by effective and ineffective helpers. In addition to our research findings, we have made many points about effective living and learning for the helper.

The findings of our research, the perspective and the model will, we hope, help to put to rest the use of gimmicks as a substitute for dedication, hard work and respect for ourselves and all our fellow men.

Confrontation is most frequently employed to degrade and defeat another human being. Growing people employ their skills to build what can grow and attack what has stopped growing. They can do this because they are truly free of the boundaries of their own skin. They experience, appreciate, love and respect life. Those only preoccupied with what is going on within the boundaries of their own skin deal only in distortions and irrelevancies and hurt.

Decency is responding without distorting. Responsibility is acting upon what we have learned when we responded. Decency and responsibility are the first steps.

Substantively, this book is based upon the work of Robert R. Carkhuff. We hope in some way it is a contribution useful to him as he continues to expand his horizons. Conceptually and programmatically, this work would not have been possible without him. We are privileged and grateful for his help and his leadership.

Rosamond Mitchell not only worked out the first scales we used to measure immediacy, but spent hundreds of hours helping to define, test and rate the variety of confrontations. Her contributions were energetic, generous and insightful.

Chapter IV is based upon much of the work by Ted W. Friel who has emerged as a leading contributor to systems related to all aspects of human resource development in general and career development in particular.

We also wish to thank Richard M. Pierce for his profound insights and skill because he knows more about the workings of helping than any of us.

Andrew H. Griffin Jr. pushed us to more useful and concrete concepts and programs so that whatever we do and say will be more useful for the individual and society. His tests, his work, energy, humanity and life is a constant reminder of what dedication is all about.

We acknowledge Ed Williams for his assistance with the analysis, and Charles Truax for making time and facilities available for the early aspects of the research.

We wish also to acknowledge the contributions of all those who pressed us to understand and re-examine what we do: David Aspy, David Berenson, Jay Griffin, Maurita Bledsoe, Bessey Ransom, and our many students.

To our wives, who enabled us to see through to helping with or without confronting, our love.

B.G.B.
K.M.M.

Springfield, Mass.
January, 1974

1

Introduction

*Most "helpers" claim to understand helpees they
have not even attended to. Most "helpers" lie!*

Any person, even a professional helper, who makes a
specialty out of confrontation or any other single
technique is:

1. *Stupid. He is committed to live life
   without learning anything more than he
   already knows.*
2. *Incompetent. He is attempting to prove
   that he can get along without substantive specialty skills.*
3. *Psychopathic. He assumes life is a game
   and the winner is the person who has
   learned the most gimmicks.*

The helper-counselor or therapist who only confronts
is a very limited helpee-client or patient: a helpee who
hopes that the best defense is good offense. What he has
not learned is that a confrontation based upon incomplete perceptions and low levels of understanding leaves
him vulnerable. His confrontations are repetitious,
impersonal and most often irrelevant. The helper who
makes a specialty of confronting is not helpful.

1. *He cannot confront constructively because he did not attend to the helpee.*
2. *He cannot confront constructively because he could not observe what he did
   not attend to.*
3. *He cannot confront constructively because he could not hear what he did
   not attend to.*
4. *He cannot confront constructively because he cannot understand what he
   did not hear, observe or attend.*
5. *He cannot confront constructively
   what he cannot understand.*

He is sick, and he is cruel because he is so completely
unaware of anyone else's existence. He calls honest
and skillful people naive, knowing full-well that their

1

emergence will expose his pathology. Most important, the confronter lacks comprehensive helping skills. Pressed to the point of full exposure, he chooses to be known as crazy or stupid rather than psychopathic and cruel. Our research demonstrates that the confronter always stops short of "going all the way", not only because he has nothing to deliver but because he must not risk being confronted by someone who will "go all the way".

Confrontation: A Perspective

Confrontation is a much talked about and much abused technique. In recent years, not only have therapists and counselors been encouraged to confront their patients and clients; their therapists and counselors, but spouses have been encouraged to confront each other; children, their parents; parents, their children; students, their teachers; teachers, their students; employees, their employers; employers, their employees; and vice versa *ad nauseum.* Based on some relevant experience and some understanding of those to be confronted, such transactions have the potential to help change behavior. In the typical instance, however, the confrontation is a simple (and simple-minded) vehicle for irresponsible venting of infantile, hostile, neurotic impulses. It is designed either to humiliate, to embarrass, or to take the focus off the inadequacies of the confronter. Most helpers simply do not have the necessary skills to discharge the responsibilities for which they are paid, whether they specialize in warmth or specialize in warmth or specialize in confronting.

Confrontation, when it is useful, is employed by those few who have earned the right to help *(Carkhuff, 1969),* those who have acquired the skills to understand themselves and others. Effective helpers can communicate an understanding at levels deeper than the helpee understands himself. Most important, however, they have systematic programs *or can develop them* to train others to live as effectively as they live; physically, emotionally, and intellectually. Without systematic

2

programs, understanding has no effect. With systematic programs, understanding increases the probability that the helpee can and will use the programs: *by programs, we simply mean systematic steps to take the helpee to where he wants to go or must go.* Without the follow-up physical, emotional and intellectual programs designed for the helpee, confrontation is at best, masturbatory and at worst, psychopathic. *In Chapter V, we present an over-all model: a program depicting the role and sequence of confrontations.*

Confrontation: Its Uses

Anything that you can do by confronting, you can do by understanding. In that respect, confrontation is not necessary, particularly if you have the time to understand the helpee. However, in the context of limited time, it may be appropriate and effective when employed by those who have earned the right to help by mastering all the relevant helping skills *(Carkhuff, 1969, 1971).*

Although confrontation, *and there are several types,* is not a major vehicle for helping, it may be employed to facilitate helper efforts to:

1. Deal with discrepant helpee behaviors.
2. Expand the interaction between himself and the helpee by creating various levels of crises in the relationship and, thus, creating a need for the helper and helpee action upon what they have come to understand about themselves and each other.
3. Make the interaction more immediate by dealing with the here and now.
4. Demonstrate that he, the helper, not only responds accurately to his world but also acts on his understanding.
5. Uncover new areas to explore; to recycle the entire helping process; to re-explore the previously-discussed but unresolved problem areas.

3

6. Demonstrate that after he has come to understand the helpee better than the helpee understands himself, his acceptance of the helpee's behavior is highly conditional.
7. Determine if the helpee is ready to act on his own behalf by being ready to be acted upon by a potent reinforcer (the helper).
8. Demonstrate that the highest level of understanding is acting upon the helpee.
9. Demonstrate that although the helping process was initially based upon the helpee's frame of reference, the initiative aspects of helping are often initially based upon the helper's frame of reference.
10. Demonstrate that he, the helper, lives more effectively than the helpee. The helper knows that once he has communicated his additive understanding of the helpee, that understanding is irrelevant unless it is acted upon. Once acted upon, understanding is again irrelevant.

Understanding is critical because it sets the stage for relevant, efficient and systematic programs of action. By itself, understanding constitutes promises without delivery. Nonetheless, it is important to emphasize that these ten functions of confrontation are possible only when confrontation is employed within the context of deep levels of accurate understanding. It is also important to emphasize that the helper must not only understand, but communicate that understanding to the helpee, *not his colleagues,* so that the helpee can act upon it. It is clear that the effective helper *person* does not employ initiative responses independent of his responsiveness and does not offer responsiveness without following it with initiative responses.

Confrontation: The role of the helper

The traditional role of the therapist as either a self-denying, warm, accepting parental surrogate or an aloof, analytic superior are absurd choices, and over the years constituted the basis for many absurd arguments. These roles, *one extreme to the other,* are as silly as suggesting that the therapist should only be assertive or only be understanding. The advocates of both extremes in roles and technique never tie their arguments to what is relevant: effectiveness. Professionals choose to defend one extreme or the other only when they are in doubt about their essential contributions and their skills to make them.

There is a growing awareness that our society and society's designated experts have not provided either the nutrition or the direction to sustain human emergence in general, and individual emergence, in particular. The therapist blames patient resistance for his or her failures; the college president blames the times for his or her failure; teachers blame the size of their class for their failure; and the parents blame their preoccupation with their career.

The evidence is overwhelming: parents, teachers, therapists, and college presidents do not have the essential skills to do their jobs. The implications of this are in evidence everywhere: we find campus disorders, under-achievement, and drug abuse. It has become vividly clear that even our moderately functioning helpers provide only a minimum contrast with a world that is cruel in its escape from individual responsibility. The minimal contrast appears only to provide apparent relief, a few techniques, and many excuses for continuing to avoid work and responsibility. Confrontation, its uses and abuses, stimulates many issues, but mainly issues of work and responsibility.

Laying a base of understanding with another person is hard work. Acting on that understanding, *confronting and developing programs,* is harder work and fixes responsibility.

5

Actually, not too many helpers really confront anyone or anything of real consequence because of their inability to confront the real issues in their own lives. They do this for the same reasons their patients avoid the real issues: lack of energy and maturity, inability to learn or work, and fear of determining their own lives. Many helpers, like their helpees, choose the certainty of being a victim over the uncertainty of growth. The most common contract established between a therapist and a patient is: "I will not **fully** expose how ineffectively you are living if you do not expose how irresponsibly I live." The irony is that for the most part, the patient knows how ineffectively he has lived and only wants to know if anyone else is aware of it. The therapist, in turn, knows how irresponsibly he lives and only wants to know if anyone else is aware of it.

It follows then, that the great majority of therapists *in our research and the literature* do whatever they can to avoid crises. If crises do occur, then therapists move to neutralize their personal responsibility, by not offering constructive follow-through. Therapists who have lived life avoiding crises can only shape their helpees to do the same. Most therapists confront when they are certain the patient is too weak and anxious to fight back; when there is no risk of personal crises for the therapist. Most confrontations are apparent confrontations, rarely are they an honest experience between the therapist and the patient.

The only relevant confrontations that lead to relevant crises are those dealing with life and death: Whether the helper has chosen to live or die, and whether the helpee has chosen to live or die. All other confrontations and crises are designed to assist the helper and the helpee avoid directly revealing their respective choices.

We cannot question the competency of a helper without questioning his competency as a person.

Unfortunately, even tragically, helping is seen and experienced as a game rather than a set of expanding substantive skills. Those who insist that helping is a game render all life a cruel, impersonal observation. In this game, the human condition is intellectualized by some, endured by most, and acted upon with honesty and responsibility by none.

2

Confrontation Research

This chapter focuses on selected attempts to specifi-
cally and operationally define confrontation in psycho-
therapy and on the definitions used in the present
research studies. There is a large body of theoretical
writings and research *e.g., (Bordin, 1955; Ellis, 1962;*
Frank, 1964; Gardner, 1964; Howe, 1962; Howe and
Pope, 1961; Kell and Neuller, 1966; Lennard and
Bernstein, 1961; Mainord, Burk, and Collins, 1965;
Mitchell, Mitchell, and Berenson, 1970; Mitchell, 1971,
Pallone and Grande, 1965; Pope and Siegman, 1962;
Thorne, 1950; and Whitaker and Malone, 1953) which
has dealt generally with therapist level of activity and
direct vs. non-directive approaches. These are certainly
forerunners to our conceptualization of confrontation
(particularly the work of Lennard and Bernstein,
Thorne, and Whitaker and Malone) but none are specific
to it.   In addition, a psychotherapy research strategy
based on the notion of the "minimally facilitative conditions" *(Carkhuff, 1969a, 1969b, 1971; Carkhuff and*
Berenson, 1967) will be formulated. Finally, prior to
investigating confrontation as both an independent and
dependent variable in process studies, the relationship
between confrontation and certain therapist demographic
variables will be examined.

Past Formulations of Confrontation

It is clear that confrontation has been accepted only
recently as a potentially helpful therapist-initiated action *(Egan, 1970).* As a consequence, operational definitions are scarce *(Berenson, Mitchell, and Laney, 1968;*
Berenson, Mitchell and Moravec, 1968; Carkhuff and
Berenson, 1967; and Mitchell and Berenson, 1970) although Egan *(1970)* presents the most complete treatment of the uses of confrontation.

Historically, Gardner *(1959, 1962, 1966)* was the first
to move beyond merely conceptual definitions to
specific therapist behaviors which define confrontation.
Gardner *(1959, 1962, 1966)* used confrontation as a
therapeutic technique which involved: **1.** a critical

8

problem recognized only vaguely or not at all by the client, but which was clearly stated by the therapist; **2.** a focus on client maladaptive *behavior,* the negative consequences of which were exaggerated by the therapist at the same time that he exaggerated possible alternatives in order to advocate possible client *actions;* and, **3.** repetitive therapist statements of the initial conflict and suggested solutions, both of which were intended to force the client to view the status quo as unacceptable and to explore new solutions to the problem.

Gardner *(1959)* viewed confrontation as a general therapeutic *technique* for resolving recalcitrant client-insight versus action difficulties, but he viewed it as only one part of the overall therapeutic process. Furthermore, he made no attempt to operationally define different types of confrontation or to measure the effectiveness of the technique. For the most part, Gardner's interaction with the patient was structured with a hypothetical framework rather than emerging from the therapist's experience of the patient. In that sense, the confrontation took the form of a game each could or could not play.

Carkhuff and Berenson *(1967)* provided a much more comprehensive view of confrontation and suggested many of the basic formulations upon which the studies to be reported in this and the following research chapters are based. They regarded confrontation as an *action initiated by the therapist*, based on his core understanding of the client, which brought the client into closer contact with himself and which forced *client action in return.* The purpose of the confrontation was to enable the client to reconcile conflicting views he had of himself so that his experience of himself and his behavior became one.

Carkhuff and Berenson described three helper-initiated confrontations which were defined in terms of three major client discrepancies: **1.** within the helpee, *his ideal versus real self;* **2.** between what the helpee said and did, *insight versus action;* and, **3.** between helpee reality and illusion, *the helper's experience of the client versus the helpee's experience of himself.* Rather than a technique, however, they saw confrontation as a helper action which reflected his overall *commitment* to helping and to his helpee and as a risk-taking behavior which gave definition to the helper as a potent role model for the helpee. The components of the helper's behavior which we have termed "commitment" and "risk-taking" will be explained in detail later in the chapter. Briefly, a confrontation is the helper's response to a basic but incorrect perception which his helpee has of himself. The helpee's distortion is so important to him and so directly attacked by the confrontation that, at the point of confronting, the helper runs the risk that the helpee will leave the relationship. The helper's commitment to the helpee and belief in himself as a helpful agent serves to reduce the anxiety associated with confronting his client. It allows him to run a risk which he perceives as not merely unavoidable but *necessary* to his helpee's growth. This was an important change in formulation since confrontation was made an integral part of the helping process and a reflection of the helper's basic view of himself as a helpful or destructive person. It left the helper responsible rather than the technique.

Confrontation as Presently Formulated

The data presented in this and the succeeding research chapters are based on a revised categorization of helper-initiated confrontations which is more explicit and more encompassing. The present formulation of confrontation includes the above-mentioned contributions. The basic difference is that *discrepancies within the helper-helpee relationship are seen as the central impediment to helpee growth.* Helper-initiated confrontations, to be most effective, must focus on discrepant helper and helpee views of the here-and-now status of the therapy relationship rather than just client intrapsychic discrepancies. Helpee intrapsychic discrepancies may still serve as the foci of confrontation, not for their own sake, but because, if basic to the helpee's central beliefs about himself, they so contaminate the therapeutic relationship that it too becomes distorted. That is, where the helpee distorts the helper and gets away with it, he is free to write the helper off as being no better than another helpee. Confrontation is an action intended to reduce that discrepancy by demanding helpee action in return *if the relationship is to continue to remain helpful.* What has been changed, then, is that confrontation focused on helpee intra-psychic discrepancies is no longer paramount. Instead, confrontation is aimed at reducing discrepancies in the helper-helpee *relationship.* In other words, basic to disordered behavior are fundamentally neurotic distortions the helpee has regarding himself and as a consequence of others.

Disordered or maladjustive behavior is fundamentally rooted in the helpee's preoccupation with irrelevancies. Most important is his preoccupation with comparisons between himself and others, particularly his helper. There is no hope that he will act more constructively for himself and others until the helper first understands him fully, communicates that understanding, and then establishes his superiority by demonstrating that he can understand the helpee better than the helpee understands himself, and that the helper, in his own life as well as in the helping session, can act on his understanding.

There are no discrepancies between the helpee's real self and how he experiences himself. The helper may see a discrepancy between how the helpee sees himself and how he could potentially see himself. However, until the helper responds fully to the helpee's experience of himself and his immediate experience with the helper, the helpee cannot entertain a more positive view of himself. Again, until these conditions are met, the helper is just another helpee. When the helpee believes himself to be inadequate, weak or evil, there will be no positive change until he knows something else is really possible: that health does exist and he cannot defeat it.

We are dealing not with helpee "myths" but·helpee distortions (or denial of what is healthy in the world) and more immediately, his distortions of a healthy helper. When the helpee loses his battle to distort and even destroy his healthy helper, the helpee wins. He is free to change his behavior. The healthy and effective helper believes fully in how he lives life. The helpee is always plagued with great doubts. It is an unequal match when the healthy helper acts on what he has come to understand.

At one level, the helpee wants help. He wants to know if there is anyone out in the world who can expose him and then train him to live more fully. At another level he goes to the helper to defeat him and to pick up a few more psychopathic games which make him less vulnerable to exposure. The real tests occur between the helper and the helpee. Hence, those helpers who are less than whole persons cannot and should not confront. Indeed, they should not be helpers. What is destructive in the helpee joins forces with what is destructive in the helper to give license to both for living destructively. The healthy and effective helper demonstrates through his impact and behavior that there is such a thing as uncompromising constructive potency.

Perhaps confrontation can be better understood if contrasted with the usual definitions of interpretation. Orthodox psychoanalytical theoreticians *e.g., (Kanzer and Blum, 1967)* argue that therapist confrontation deals with obvious resistances in order to pave the way for interpretations which deal with *deeper (unconcious)* material. It is also usually argued that confrontation helps the client to *see* his problems or conflicts whereas interpretations *explain* the problems or conflicts. We see the relationship between interpretation and confrontation in a very different light. First, interpretations emphasize the *necessity* of insight in order to change, a requirement which has been seriously and successfully dismissed *(Carkhuff, 1969; Carkhuff and Berenson, 1967; Frank, 1961; Gardner, 1964; and Hobbs, 1962)*. Second, interpretations also involve historical reconstruction, a requirement that is taken even less seriously today than insight *(Hobbs, 1962)*. Whether insight or reconstruction is the goal, the process is based on poor levels of understanding *(Carkhuff and Berenson, 1967)*.

What more orthodox therapists do not understand is that confrontation can lead to client insight. Whether or not insight is a *necessary* ingredient to change, it may be helpful in initiating behavior or more likely, in integrating new behaviors after they occur. Nevertheless, there is no reason why confrontation should preclude insight or further explanation. Furthermore, confrontation demonstrates the helper's commitment to his helpee and himself in a way that helper-initiated interpretations cannot. Interpretations, no matter how deep and dynamic the material focused upon, are passive, disinterested, "objective" responses that tell the client nothing about his therapist's way of life. Confrontation is an active, evaluative, "subjective" response which offers the helpee much-needed feedback about his impact on his helper, *helpee potency,* and about his helper's concern and commitment, *helper potency.*

Singer *(1965)* has offered an analysis of confrontation and interpretation which, although incomplete as far as we are concerned, may make therapist-initiated confrontations more palatable for orthodox psychotherapists. He emphasizes the importance of confrontation in the on-going therapeutic relationship by asserting that confrontation allows the helpee to see that his helper sees him as he really is and yet is able to care for him. This reduces the helpee's anxiety since he no longer has to behave, in the therapy hour, under the assumption that if his helper really knew him he would reject him. Singer also argues that therapists who do not confront their clients are likely to be seen as weak and foolish since clients know, at some level, that much of what they say is erroneous and *should be confronted.* Our position is not that the helper sees who the helpee really is and still cares for him, but rather the helper will not, in the long run, accept the helpee at less than he can be.

Five major types of confrontation were delineated: Experiential, Didactic, Strength, Weakness, and Encouragement to Action. *Experiential* confrontation is defined as the helper's specific response to any discrepancy between the helpee and helper's experiencing of the helper-helpee relationship, or to any discrepancy between the helpee's overt statement about himself and the helpee's inner, covert experience of himself, or to any discrepancy between the helpee and helper's subjective experience of either the helper or helpee. A *Didactic* confrontation is defined as the helper's direct clarification of the helpee's misinformation or lack of information about relatively *objective* aspects of his world or the therapeutic relationship. This type of confrontation may include the helper's efforts to offer the helpee information based on test data; data about some aspect of the world; or details about the structure and function of the therapy process. It will become clear that *Didactic* confrontations may not share with the other types of confrontation the same dynamic intensity and risk-taking components. They are less often associated with strongly held distortions but, in our conceptual framework, they fill a logical vacuum. In addition, they may serve to orient the helpee to the therapeutic process and help him to be prepared for more central and dynamic confrontations. It also should be noted that *Experiential* and *Didactic* confrontations may be difficult to differentiate when the confrontation is aimed at certain distortions the helpee may have about his significant others. If the helper focuses on the helpee's presumably incorrect interpretation of another person's behavior, for example, we have termed that a *Didactic* confrontation. On the other hand, if the helper uses the helpee's incorrect interpretation of another's behavior in order to focus on distortions held by the helpee about *himself* which led to such an interpretation

14

we have called that an *Experiential* confrontation. Confrontation of *Strength* refers to an experiential confrontation which focuses on the helpee's resources. *Weakness* refers to an experiential confrontation which focuses on the helpee's liabilities or pathology. Finally, *Encouragement to Action* involves the helper's pressing the helpee to act on his world in some reasonable, appropriate, and constructive manner; and discouraging a passive stance toward life.

We initially had the impression that certain confrontations were inherently "better", i.e., more therapeutic, than others. We now regard this notion as fairly naive: not only as it refers to confrontation but also as it applies to any behavior which occurs in helping. Our understanding of confrontation leads us to believe that any confrontation can be beneficial or harmful as a function of other helper skills which tend to make him helpful or harmful. In addition, we believe that confrontation must also be evaluated as a function of time, a variable of tremendous importance which largely has been overlooked in psychotherapy research.

For example, a large number of studies *(Carkhuff, 1969; 1971)* have demonstrated that high levels of empathic understanding relate significantly to positive gain for the helpee, and, that over time, the helpee does move toward the helper's level of functioning. However, Carkhuff *(1969)* points out that moderate or interchangeable levels of empathic understanding are initially most facilitative. He goes on to demonstrate that the highest levels of empathic understanding are useful only after the helpee demonstrates he is able to sustain exploration of his experience without interchangeable helper empathic responses. It is clear that if the helper provides "high" *additive* levels of understanding too early, the helpee is less likely to use it because the helper has yet to establish himself as an important person in the life of the helpee. In addition, the helpee has not explored his experience fully enough to provide the information for accurate additive helper responses.

Attempted additive responses before the helpee can provide himself with interchangeable levels of understanding are often faulty, vague and ingenuine. The same may be said for the use of confrontations before an additive base of understanding has been established by the helper. Only when the helper has demonstrated that he can significantly add to the helpee's understanding of himself can he, the helper, entertain employing confrontations.

We are of the opinion that confrontation cannot be viewed simply as a specific in-therapy behavior without consideration of other, more broadly based characteristics, which define the helper-as-person. In other words, confrontation, like interpretation or reflection, is not an inherently helpful behavior that should be used at any and all opportunities. Instead, it is a specific in-therapy behavior which gains its effectiveness from the point in helping when it is used and, more importantly, from the human, nourishing characteristics of the helper. Theoreticians as well as practitioners are concerned presently with the relative passivity inherent in much helping. On the other hand, action for its own sake, and particularly in the hands of a hostile, distant and/or ingenuine helper, is no substitute for a healthy, humane, nurturant human being. Action, precipitously triggered and uncaringly reinforced, may be more harmful than doing nothing at all.

The remainder of this chapter is given over to a detailed account of the research design and to a study of the relationships between certain helper demographic variables and confrontation. The research chapter which follows will investigate the relationship between confrontation and helper-helpee variables which are more clinical in nature and which are more relevant to the effectiveness of the therapeutic endeavor.

The studies to be reported in this and the following chapter are based on data collected from tape-recorded first helping interviews of 56 helpers, professional counselors, and therapists representing the fields of clinical and counseling psychology, psychiatry, and social work, as well as advanced graduate students in clinical and counseling psychology. Table 1 provides demographic information describing the helpers in the sample by discipline, orientation, type of practice, experience, sex, and type of helpee.

Table 1
Summary of Helpers' Characteristics

	N
Discipline	**N**
Clinical Psychology	15
Counseling Psychology	6
Psychiatry	12
Social Work	7
Clinical Psychology Students	6
Counseling Psychology	10
Orientation*	**N**
Analytically-oriented	23
Client-centered	8
Eclectic	8
Relationship	16
Practice	**N**
Counseling Center	23
Hospital	33
Experience *Excluding Students*	**N**
Less Experienced	27
More Experienced	13
Sex	**N**
Female	6
Male	50

One helper could not be identified by orientation. Consequently the number of helpers is 55.

Helpees ranged from minimally disturbed college students to hospitalized chronic schizophrenics. Of the 56 helpees, 23 were seen in university counseling centers and 33 were seen in hospital settings. Formal diagnoses were not available for the students, but on the basis of the tape recordings, most appeared to be mildly to moderately disturbed neurotics although a handful seemed more disturbed and would be best described as ranging from neurotic character disorders to ambulatory schizophrenics. The hospital helpees were either acute or chronic schizophrenics with the exception of approximately five whom we diagnosed as sociopathic personalities with alcohol or drug addictions as primary symptoms. The tape recordings were collected on the basis of availability from a number of different institutions across the country.

The basic design of the studies is based on a larger number of studies summarized by Carkhuff *(1969)* and Carkhuff and Berenson *(1967)* and Truax and Carkhuff *(1967)* which clearly demonstrates that the helper facilitative conditions of **Empathic Understanding, Positive Regard, Genuineness, and Concreteness** are related significantly to positive helpee outcome. It is our belief that these conditions reflect rather broad and relatively permanent helper personality characteristics as well as interpersonal skills. There is ample evidence to suggest that these or similar characteristics facilitate growth in a number of other areas in addition to helping; e.g., **1.** teacher—student relations *(Aspy, 1965; Truax and Tatum, 1965; Wagner and Mitchell, 1969)*, and, **2.** parent—child relations *(Bateson, Jackson and Weakland, 1956; Freeman and Grayson, 1955; Mark, 1953; Meyer and Karon, 1967; Mitchell, 1968, 1969)*.

In other words, these facilitative conditions, first operationally defined in the helping relationship, are not specific to helping or to the helper — helpee relationship. In fact, it is quite likely that these conditions lent themselves so readily to measurement and were so clearly demonstrated to be related to helpee outcome precisely because they reflect broad, easily discerned, and generally effective personality characteristics of helpful persons who are or can be effective in a number of disparate situations. Nevertheless, it is also reasonable to expect that there are effective helper behaviors which are more specific to the helping.

The data supplied by Carkhuff and Berenson *(1967)*, Truax and Carkhuff *(1967)*, and Carkhuff *(1969)* also strongly suggest that helping can be "for better or for worse". That is, the helpees of some helpers improve while the helpees of other helpers show no improvement or actual deterioration. On this basis, Kiesler *(1966)* has cautioned against continuing the "therapist uniformity myth", that all helpers are quite similar and relatively equally helpful. It is very likely that the same behavior has very different consequences in the hands of a helper who offers high levels of the facilitative conditions in comparison to a helper who consistently offers low conditions. Consequently, not only are helpers and helping not unitary variables, but neither are those more specific behaviors usually associated with helping *e.g., confrontation, interpretation, reflecting, etc.*

This is one reason that a different strategy than is usually employed in psychotherapy research was devised to study helper confrontation. Briefly, the tape-recorded first helping interviews of the 56 professional helpers were rated on Empathic Understanding *(Berenson and Carkhuff, 1964);* Positive Regard *(Carkhuff and Berenson, 1964);* Genuineness *(Carkhuff, 1964a);* and Concreteness *(Carkhuff, 1964b).* Helpers were then categorized as high and low facilitators on the basis of a mean facilitative score and, subsequently, most analyses of confrontation took this basic categorization of helpers into account.

In addition, in the attempt to control for the "therapist uniformity myth", there is a second, and more compelling reason for fitting the facilitative conditions into our study of confrontation. To date, no other helper variables have been subjected to a comparable programmatic research effort or related as consistently to positive helpee outcome. The scales used to measure these conditions have proven to be reliable

(Carkhuff, 1969; Carkhuff and Berenson, 1967; Truax and Carkhuff, 1967) and predictive of helpee outcome in a large number of studies involving helpers of vastly different orientations and helpees representing almost every diagnostic category. The scales used in this series to measure these helper facilitative conditions are reported by Carkhuff *(1969)*. Essentially, they were five-point scales that ranged from level 1 — *least effective* to level 5 — *most effective*, with level 3 being *minimally effective*.

Table 2
Mean Empathy, Positive Regard,
Genuineness, Concreteness and Facilitative Index
for High and Low Functioning Helpers

Helpers	Empathy	Positive Regard	Genuineness	Concreteness	Facilitative Index
High Functioning N = 13	3.19	3.32	3.51	3.07	3.27
Low Functioning N = 43	1.55	1.59	1.53	1.66	1.58

The 56 first helping interviews were rated independently on Empathic Understanding, Positive Regard, Genuineness, Concreteness or Specificity of Expression, and Depth of Self-Exploration *(Carkhuff, 1969)* by two experienced clinicians with eight and four years of post-doctoral experience, respectively.

Table 2 indicates the mean score for the high and low facilitative helpers on Empathy, Positive Regard, Genuineness, Concreteness and the Facilitative Index. T-tests for independent measures and unequal N's indicated that the two groups of helpers were significantly different on all five measures $p < .001$.

A second pair of independent judges then listened to each of the 56 helping tapes in its entirety and noted the frequency of each type of confrontation. A confrontation was accepted only if both judges agreed on its presence and type.

20

Reliability estimates for each of the two raters for each of the helper facilitative conditions were: Empathy, .90, .88; Positive Regard, .92, .89; Genuineness .90, .85; Concreteness, .89, .84; and Depth of Helpee Self-Exploration, .90, .95. The intercorrelations between the raters were: Empathy, .96; Positive Regard, .96; Genuineness, .80; Concreteness, .88; and Depth of Helpee Self-Exploration, .76.

Scores were based on ratings of 3-minute segments taken randomly from each fifth portion of the hour. The ratings of both judges were averaged to obtain a mean Empathy, Positive Regard, Genuineness, and Concreteness score for each helper and a mean Depth of Self-Exploration score for each helpee. Subsequently, each helper was categorized as a high or low facilitator on the basis of a mean Facilitative Index derived from averaging the mean Empathy, Positive Regard, Genuineness, and Concreteness scores. Helpers who averaged 2.5 and above were classified as high; helpers below 2.5 were classified as low facilitators. This categorization resulted in 13 high functioning and 43 low functioning helpers.

The decision to use a mean facilitative index of 2.5 to differentiate between high and low functioning helpers was based on research data which suggest the notion of "minimally facilitative conditions" *(Carkhuff, 1969; and, Carkhuff and Berenson, 1967).* Essentially, a number of studies have indicated that in order to produce positive helpee outcome, helpers must offer at least interchangeable, *level 3,* levels of facilitative dimensions *(Carkhuff, 1969).*

Tables 3, 4, and 5 indicate the distributions of the different confrontations as a function of helper discipline, orientation, and experience, respectively. It is clear from these data that the distributions of confrontations create serious problems for statistical analyses of the data. Confrontation, based on the sample used in the present series of studies, appears to be a relatively rare occurrence within the first interview, particularly as a function of certain helper categorizations; confrontation categories are not normally distributed as a function of *any* helper classification system; across helper categorizations, heterogeneity of variance is marked. Since we have no reason to believe that our sample is markedly dissimilar from the population of helpers who represent the various disciplines who are employed in hospitals and university counseling centers, we feel that this is the ecological nature of confrontation.

Nevertheless, the ecological characteristics of confrontation do play havoc with usual statistical procedures. Generally, we have taken the position that nominal scale data can be analyzed by parametric methods *(Cohen, 1966)* if we maintain a somewhat conservative position in interpreting statistically significant differences. For example, for our purposes, a significant **F**-ratio means "more or less than" and nothing more. In addition, for most analyses, we transformed the confrontation frequencies by: $\sqrt{X+10}$ where **X** = the number of confrontations. On the other hand, we have also taken the position that these same ecological characteristics can mask "significant" differences. Consequently, on occasion we have highlighted differences which do not reach statistical significance since the growing ecological orientation in psychology suggests that the truly important "in vivo" helping variables may be, by their very nature, statistically "difficult".

Helper Discipline

Table 3 indicates the number and types of confrontation by helper discipline. Prior analyses had indicated that the disciplines were not significantly different on empathy, positive regard, genuineness, or concreteness. One-way analyses of variance for unequal **N**'s were used on the transformed data to compare the five disciplines on each type and total number of confrontations. None of the comparisons produced a significant **F**-ratio and, consequently, it was concluded that discipline and confrontation were unrelated. Although the disciplines were not significantly different, it is clear from Table 3 that the graduate students offered many more **Experiential, Didactic, Strength,** and **Action** confrontations than their professional counterparts. Perhaps the most parsimonious explanation is that the younger helpers are responding to compelling contemporary exhortations to be more personally involved and action-oriented than helpers have been in the past *(Carkhuff, 1969; Carkhuff and Berenson, 1967; Ellis, 1962; Gardner, 1964; Lennard and Bernstein, 1961; Thorne; 1950; and Whitaker and Malone, 1953).*

Table 3
Frequency and Type of Confrontation
by Helper Discipline

| Discipline | Confrontation | | | | | |
	Experiential	Didactic	Strength	Weakness	Action	Total
Clinical Psy (N=15)	22	3	2	11	3	41
Counseling Psy (N=6)	7	7	3	4	1	22
Psychiatry (N=12)	8	2	0	9	2	21
Social Work (N=7)	14	6	0	6	1	27
Graduate Stud. (N=16)	45	13	6	7	9	80
Totals	96	31	11	37	16	191

Helper Orientation

The distribution of confrontations as a function of helper orientations — *analytically-oriented, helpee-centered, eclectric and relationship* — were categorized by at least one and often two colleagues who knew them. Admittedly a hazardous method, the data reflect differences which appear at least tentatively meaningful although a more rigorous replication of these findings is obviously necessary.

Duncan's multiple range test for unequal N's *(1957)* was used to compare the orientation groups only if a previously computed F-ratio, using a one way analysis of variance, was significant. F-ratios significant at or

23

beyond the .01 level were obtained for Experiential, Didactic, Strength and total number of confrontations F's = *7.135, 7.331, 4.903 and 8.756, respectively.* Significant F-ratios were not obtained for either Weakness or Action confrontations.

Table 4
Frequency and Type of Confrontation
by Helper Orientation

| Orientation | Confrontation | | | | | |
	Experiential	Didactic	Strength	Weakness	Action	Totals
Analytic *(N=23)*	9	3	0	15	4	31
Client-Centered *(N=8)*	13	1	2	6	1	23
Eclectic *(N=7)*	15	2	0	10	2	29
Relationship *(N=16)*	64	27	9	3	10	113
Totals	101	33	11	34	17	196

Additional analyses indicated that the relationship-oriented helpers offered more Experiential and total number of confrontations than other orientation groups. There were no significant differences among analytic, helpee-centered, and eclectic helpers.

The relationship helpers also offered significantly more *Didactic* confrontations than all other orientation $p<.01$ and significantly more Strength confrontations than the analytic and eclectic helpers $p<.01$. The relationship and helpee-centered helpers did not differ significantly on Strength confrontations. Neither were there significant differences among the analytic, helpee-centered, and eclectic helpers.

To summarize the findings with respect to helper orientation, all the significant differences found for *Experiential, Didactic,* and *Strength* confrontations were due to the fact that the relationship-oriented helpers offered significantly more of these confrontations than the other orientations with the exception of the helpee-centered helpers on *Strength* confrontations.

It is difficult to evaluate the findings for helper orientation. At best, the results certainly reflect what each orientation professes to do in helping. This would seem to be particularly true for the relationship helpers

24

who confront more often than any other orientation on all confrontations except *Weakness* but also provide higher average levels of the other dimensions. The analytically-oriented helpers listen more, perhaps making cover diagnostic judgements, since they offer the least number of *Experiential* confrontations. They also tend, unfortunately in our view, to focus on helpee pathology with a consistency that has recently drawn fire from a number of quarters *e.g., (Cowan, Gardner, and Zax, 1967).*

Helper Experience

Because our sample includes advanced level graduate students, it was decided to investigate the relationship between confrontation and level of helper experience with and without the students. Helpers, *excluding the 16 graduate students,* were categorized as less, *0 - 5 years,* and more, *6 - 15 years,* experienced. These criteria had been used by Strupp *(1962)* and reflect a traditional and perhaps somewhat arbitrary way of classifying helper experience. Experience level represented post-doctoral experience for the psychologists, and post-residency and post-MSW experience for the psychiatrists and social workers, respectively. The classification resulted in 27 less and 13 more experienced helpers. Independent t-tests for unequal N's indicated that there were no significant differences between the two groups of helpers on any of the confrontation types or on the total number of confrontations.

When the graduate students were included, the N was large enough to categorize the helpers into both more and less experience and high and low facilitative on the basis of a mean facilitative index of 2.0. The mean facilitative index of 2.0 was used instead of 2.5 because it was felt that the notion of "minimally facilitative conditions" was not inimical to experience level and because use of such a cut-off index resulted in approximately equal cell N's. In this situation some of the psychologists, psychiatrists, and social workers who were placed in the "more experienced" category had had four instead of six or more years of post-terminal degree or post-residency experience. 2 X 2 factorial analyses for unequal **N**'s by the unweighted means method, were computed separately for **Experiential, Didactic, Strength, Weakness, Action** and total number of confrontations.

TABLE 5
FREQUENCY AND TYPE OF CONFRONTATION BY HELPER LEVEL OF EXPERIENCE AND FACILITATIVE INDEX

Confrontation	High Experience *(n=28)*		Low Experience *(n=28)*	
	High Facilitator *(n=10)*	Low Facilitator *(n=18)*	High Facilitator *(n=12)*	Low Facilitator *(n=16)*
Experiential	33	12	50	7
Didactic	11	6	15	4
Strength	5	0	5	1
Weakness	0	22	6	7
Action	3	2	5	7
Total	52	42	81	26

Analyses of the data indicated that although helper facilitative conditions had a significant main effect on **Experiential** $F = 23.171$, $p < .0001$, **Didactic** $F = 6.788$, $p<.01$, **Strength** $F = 10.089$, $p<.005$, and the total number of confrontations $F = 15.438$, $p<.001$, helper experience did not provide a significant main effect on any of these confrontations $F = 3.745$, $p<.05$. It can be seen from Table 5 that helpers with a Facilitative Index of 2.0 and above offered significantly more **Experiential, Didactic, Strength,** and total number of confrontations than low facilitative helpers. This is an extremely important finding and confirms the research strategy of categorizing helpers as high and low facilitators even when the notion of "minimally facilitative conditions" was not adhered to. Clearly, these two groups of helpers are different. From Table 5 it can be seen also that the significant interaction effect on **Weakness** confrontations was due to the fact that the high experience-low facilitative helpers offered more of such confrontations than the other groups.

Disregarding statistical analyses, inspection of Table 5

indicates that the low experience-low facilitative helpers offered a particularly disturbing combination of few Experiential and Strength confrontations and a relatively greater number of Action confrontations. It seems reasonable to speculate that at least within the first interview, the combination of relatively little experience, low facilitative conditions, relatively few Experiential and Strength confrontations, and relatively more Action confrontations could lead to marked helpee deterioration particularly to the degree that such helpers are successful in having their helpers act on their significant others. Such action, by definition, would be ill-timed and without appropriate supportive basis. Although we do not have such evidence for this group of helpers, we feel strongly that the particular integration of helper personality and behavioral characteristics which describe these 16 helpers may be particularly destructive and may offer further and more behaviorly-oriented evidence for the "for better or worse" hypothesis. It should also be noted that the more experienced low facilitators, when they confronted, offered almost twice as many Weakness confrontations as any other category; indeed over half of all their confrontations focused on helpee pathology. This also strikes us as specific in-therapy behavior which would lead to helpee deterioration. This would seem particularly true in the absence of minimally facilitative conditions despite our suspicion that focusing on *helpee pathology* may not be seen by many *therapy teachers* and/or supervisors as particularly destructive behavior.

To summarize the data on helper experience, it appears that as defined in this series of studies and for this sample of helpers' experience, per se, had little effect on confrontation. Of much greater importance, however, was the finding that helper levels of the facilitative conditions had a significant effect on all confrontations except Action.

Helper Sex

Of the 56 helpers in the sample, only six were female. Since comparing all the male with all the female helpers would result in grossly unequal N's, six male helpers matched separately on Empathy, Positive Regard, Genuineness, and Concreteness were compared with the six female helpers. Use of dependent t-tests indicated that there were no significant differences on number or type of confrontation as a function of sex.

Concluding Remarks

At different stages in this chapter we have attempted to summarize the findings. Some concluding remarks are in order. There was a significant relationship between helper facilitative conditions, which had been related previously to positive helpee outcome, and helper-initiated confrontation. This finding justifies our general research strategy and at least suggests that confrontation may be related to helpee outcome although certainly in no simple fashion.

The statistically significant confrontation differences we have reported as a function of helper orientation and the differences between professional and graduate student helpers are of ecological interest at this point in time, and may only reflect ideological beliefs of those groups. Over the course of helping, experienced and effective helpers come to behave more like each other. The effects of training, so patently obvious in the first interview, decrease markedly over time as a function of the idiosyncratic, helper-helpee relationship. On the other hand, it may well be that, for ineffective helpers, training effects are only minimally influenced by the waxing and waning of each helping relationship and that, like helpees, early experiences are not easily changed as a function of subsequent different relationships. It is also important to keep in mind that other studies point out that low functioning helpers offer their "best" during the first few minutes of the first hours; thereafter, everything is down hill *(Carkhuff, 1969)*.

28

3

Confrontation

This chapter will focus on the differential distributions of confrontation as a function of categorizing the 56 helpers into high-and low-functioning groups on the basis of "minimally facilitative conditions". In addition, helpees were categorized by institutional setting as either university counseling center students or hospitalized schizophrenics and as high or low self-exploring as a function of Client Depth of Self-Exploration in Inter-Personal Processes *(Carkhuff, 1969).* Confrontation was subsequently examined as a function of these helpee categorizations.

Correlational Analyses

Before turning to these process studies, we should like to present the correlation relationships among the data. Tables 6 and 7 are correlational matrices for high and low functioning helpers, respectively, which indicate the Pearson product-moment correlations *based on the transformation: X x 10* between each of the helper facilitative conditions and each confrontation category as well as the Facilitative Index and the total number of confrontations.

The matrices for high- and low-functioning helpers were computed separately since prior analyses indicated that the two groups of helpers were significantly different on Empathy, Positive Regard, Genuineness, Concreteness, and the Facilitative Index. Consequently, we expected that one over-all matrix which included the data on all 56 helpers would be misleading if not completely irrelevant, and that separate matrices would generate quite different relationships among variables, and more accurately characterize the integration of skills and behaviors which are unique to these two distinct groups of helpers. The data in Table 6 are based on the 13 high-functioning helpers since each offered at least one confrontation, but the data in Table 7 are based on 32 of the 43 low-functioning helpers since eleven of these helpers offered no confrontations.

Table 6
Correlation Matrix for High-Functioning Helpers on Frequency and Types of Confrontation and Facilitative Conditions

	Empathy	Positive Regard	Genuineness	Concreteness	Facilitative Index	Experiential	Didactic	Strength	Weakness	Action
Empathy										
Positive Regard	.69***									
Genuineness	.41	.87***								
Concreteness	.44	.15	.05							
Facilitative Index	.73***	.98****	.92***	.20						
Experiential	.47	.77****	.58**	-.17	.69***					
Didactic	-.07	.29	.14	.15	.16	.33				
Strength	.14	.10	.19	-.16	.16	-.28	-.17			
Weakness	-.01	.12	-.10	-.25	-.01	.49*	.25	-.31		
Action	.46	.21	.17	.24	.29	.19	-.09	.23	.25	
Total Confrontations	.43	.76***	.55*	-.07	.66**	.90****	.61**	-.10	.53*	.35

*p < .10
**p < .05
***p < .01

Table 7
Correlation Matrix for Low-Functioning Helpers on Frequency and Types of Confrontation and Facilitative Conditions

	Empathy	Positive Regard	Genuineness	Concreteness	Facilitative Index	Experiential	Didactic	Strength	Weakness	Action
Empathy										
Positive Regard	.79***									
Genuineness	.77***	.87***								
Concreteness	.88***	.83***	.81***							
Facilitative Index	.91***	.95***	.93***	.90***						
Experiential	.34*	.25	.25	.35*	.29					
Didactic	-.01	-.01	-.08	-.11	-.03	-.06				
Strength	.23	.33*	.54***	.26	.39**	.04	.16			
Weakness	-.02	-.15	-.07	-.08	-.08	-.05	-.19	-.22		
Action	-.05	.03	.16	-.07	.04	.44**	.25	.39**	-.14	
Total Confrontations	.21	.08	.17	.11	.15	.70***	.20	.18	.46***	.62*

* $p < .10$
** $p < .05$
*** $p < .01$

31

Relationships Among the Facilitative Conditions

With regard to the facilitative conditions only, an important difference emerged between the high- and low-functioning helpers. Helpers who had a Facilitative Index of 2.5 and above offered the different facilitative conditions of Empathy, Positive Regard, Genuineness, and Concreteness to their helpees somewhat more independently than do low-functioning helpers. In other words, although Empathy, Positive Regard, and Genuineness were correlated significantly and positively with the Facilitative Index $p<.01$, Concreteness was correlated significantly with none of the other conditions nor with the Facilitative Index. Furthermore, although the correlations between Empathy and Positive Regard, and Positive Regard and Genuineness were positive and significant $p<.01$, no significant relationship was found between Empathy and Genuineness. On the other hand, all the facilitative conditions offered by the low-functioning helpers were significantly related to each other $p<.01$. In contrast to the low-functioning helpers, the high-functioning helpers' levels of Concreteness were offered independently of the other conditions, and the levels of Empathy and Genuineness were offered independently of each other.

It is difficult to interpret such correlational data, but one hypothesis is that the high-functioning helpers were able to appraise individual helpee's needs more accurately than low-functioning helpers, and perhaps were more responsive to these needs. As a result, they offered differential levels of the facilitative conditions partially as a function of differential helpee needs and time. That is, over time they offer higher and higher levels. Low-functioning helpers, on the other hand, appear to have offered the same low levels of conditions in a consistent but indiscriminate fashion, and apparently, independently of the idiosyncratic helper-helpee relationship, over time they provide lower and lower levels of these dimensions.

Relationship between Confrontation and the Facilitative Conditions

Examination of the correlations between the facilitative conditions and confrontation highlight differences between high and low-functioning helpers. Among those helpers with a Facilitative Index of 2.5 and above, the number of **Experiential** confrontations was significantly and positively correlated with Genuineness $p<.05$, and with Positive Regard and the Facilitative Index $p<.01$. There was also a moderate and positive, although not significant, relationship between the number of confrontations and Positive Regard $p<.01$, Genuineness $p<.10$, and the Facilitative Index $p<.05$, and a moderate but not significantly positive relationship between the total number of confrontations and Empathy. Similarly, there were significant positive correlations between the total number of confrontations and Positive Regard $p<.01$, Genuineness $p<.10$, and Facilitative Index $p<.05$, and a moderate but not significantly positive relationship between the total number of confrontations and Empathy. No doubt the relationships between the total number of confrontations and the facilitative conditions were largely a function of the findings for the Experiential Confrontations. As far as the high-functioning helpers were concerned, the only other somewhat substantial correlations were small to moderate but consistently positive correlations between **Action** confrontations and all the facilitative conditions, particularly Empathy. This may be due to the fact that for the high-functioning helper, action may be premature or tentative during the first helping session.

The number of **Experiential** confrontations offered by low-functioning in contrast to high-functioning helpers was only moderately correlated with the facilitative conditions, particularly with Empathy and Concreteness $p<.10$. However, the relationships found for the high-functioning helpers between **Action** and total number of confrontations and the facilitative conditions did not hold for the low-functioning helpers. Interestingly, unlike the high-functioning helpers, the number of **Strength** confrontations offered by the low-functioning helpers was significantly, and positively, correlated with Positive Regard $p<.10$, Genuineness $p<.01$, and the Facilitative Index $p<.05$. Like the high-functioning helpers, there was no substantial correlations between any of the facilitative conditions and either **Didactic** or **Weakness** confrontations. It must be emphasized that few confrontations were correlated with low levels of dimensions for the lows.

To summarize the intercorrelations among the facilitative conditions and confrontation, it was found that for the high-functioning helpers, Positive Regard, Genuineness and the Facilitative Index were significantly and positively related to both **Experiential** and the total number of confrontations. There were small to moderate positive correlations between the number of **Action** confrontations and all the facilitative conditions. Positive Regard, Genuineness, and the Facilitative Index were predictive of both **Experiential** and total number of confrontations, and there was a consistently positive but statistically insignificant relationship between the facilitative conditions and **Action** confrontations. For low-functioning helpers, there was only a moderate relationship between the number of **Experiential** confrontations and the facilitative conditions, particularly Empathy and Concreteness $p<.10$. The facilitative conditions were related positively to the number of **Strength** confrontations, particularly Positive Regard $p<.10$, Genuineness $p<.01$, and the Facilitative Index $p<.05$.

Correlational data do not explain but merely describe. Thus, it is difficult to infer much more from the correlations between the facilitative conditions and confrontation except that, clearly, the inter-relationships among the variables are different for high- and low-functioning helpers. By way of explanation, it seems plausible enough to infer that the correlational data suggest that the two groups of helpers were quite different in the way they combined and integrated their in-therapy behaviors and that future research should focus on the relationships between differential combinations of these variables and helpee outcome rather than continuing to focus on variables in a singular fashion. The other point which may be made is that the facilitative conditions were more strongly related to confrontation for the high-than for the low-functioning helpers. There is, in general, a higher order of relationships among all dimensions of helping for higher functioning helpers. Low-functioning helpers generally demonstrate that their behaviors are not related or that we are correlating low levels of all dimensions *(Carkhuff, 1969).*

Relationships among the Confrontation Categories

Finally, attention was focused on the relationships among the confrontation categories. Of particular interest, for both high- and low-functioning helpers, was the fact that the confrontation categories appear to be relatively independent of each other. For example, among high-functioning helpers, although **Experiential** $p<.01$, **Didactic** $p<.05$, and **Weakness** $p<.10$ confrontations were correlated significantly and positively with the total number of confrontations, the only other significant correlation was between the number of **Experiential** and **Weakness** confrontations $p<.10$. Similarly, for the low-functioning helpers, although **Experiential**, **Weakness** and **Action** confrontations were correlated positively and significantly with the total number of confrontations $p<.01$, the only other significant correlations were between **Experiential** and **Action** $p<.05$ and **Experiential** and **Strength** confrontations $p<.05$. Again, we are describing the relationship among low levels of the measures.

This is in sharp contrast to the relationships among the facilitative conditions where, among the high-functioning helpers, for example, 50% of the total

35

number of correlations computed between the facilitative conditions reached the .01 level of significance. Between confrontation categories, on the other hand, 27% of the correlations were significant at the .10 level of significance and only 7% at the .01 level of significance. Similarly, among the low-functioning helpers, 100% of the correlations computed between the facilitative conditions were significant at the .01 level of significance whereas 33% of the correlations computed between the confrontation categories were significant at the .05 level of significance and only 20% at the .01 level of significance. It would seem that types of confrontations, as defined in this series of studies, reflect fairly independent helper behaviors for both high and low-functioning helpers.

Setting aside the correlations between the different confrontation categories and the total number of confrontations since these are spuriously high, relationships between other confrontation categories should be noted. The significant relationship between the number of **Experiential** and **Weakness** confrontations $p<.10$ was the only other significant correlation between confrontations for the high-functioning helpers. Apparently these helpers focused on helpees' disordered behavior as part of their attempt to develop and intensify the helping relationship. On the other hand, although we believe that **Experiential** and **Strength** confrontations would be significantly, and positively, correlated over the course of successful helping, within the first helping session they were negatively correlated for high-functioning helpers and were apparently unrelated among low-functioning helpers. As might have been expected from the definitions of **Strength** and **Weakness** confrontations, there was a slightly negative correlation between these confrontation categories for both high and low-functioning helpers.

Another finding was the positive and significant correlation between **Experiential** and **Action** confrontations for the low-functioning helpers. Apparently, these helpers combined confrontations which focused on discrepancies in the helping relationship with exhortations for the helpee to act. It may be, however, that the number of defenses and discrepancies which can be cleared away in the first helping hour are rather few and that, as a result, the helpee has not yet given up the appropriate conviction that he cannot be helped by a low-funcitoning helper. Under these conditions, **Action** confrontations may be premature and inappropriate and may undo or weaken whatever benefit may have been gained from the use of **Experiential** confrontations. Further, the action confrontations are the dominant source for all helpees of low-functioning helpers. Other research *(Carkhuff and Berenson, 1967; Truax and Carkhuff, 1967; and Truax and Mitchell, 1968)* has demonstrated that low-functioning helpers produce either no change or helpee deterioration. Our hypothesis, that **Action** confrontations within the first interview may undo **Experiential** confrontations and lead the helpee into precipitous behavior which would only confirm his belief that he and his significant others are impotent, may pinpoint a specific helper behavior that leads to either no change or deterioration.

Finally, it should be noted that the **Strength** and **Action** confrontations of low-functioning helpers were significantly correlated *p<.05.* This should have been expected from the way in which these confrontations had been defined, although the relationship was not significant for high-functioning helpers. The low-functioning helpers respond to strengths that are often weaknesses and weaknesses that are strengths.

The point is that the low-functioning helper is frequently a very poor discriminator because his repertoire of responses is so small and of such poor quality. He is, in fact, not certain about what is adaptive *Strength* and what is maladaptive *Weakness.* If the helper does not have a functional repertoire of responses for helping, he is not fit to make the judgement. If he does act, he compounds the helpee's problem by encouraging the helpee to act as he does: inappropriately.

Summary of the Correlational Analyses

Two findings from the correlation data are of particular importance and bear repeating. First, high and low-functioning helpers were not only significantly different in a statistical sense, but they were also quite different in the way their facilitative conditions and confrontation behaviors were interrelated. In other words, the two groups of helpers appear to be different in complex structural ways which will be examined later in more detail. Second, unlike the facilitative conditions of Empathy, Positive Regard, Genuineness, and Concreteness, the confrontation categories seem to reflect fairly independent helper behaviors, at least during the first helping interview with the qualifications which follow.

Presence and Type of Confrontation as a Function of Helper-Facilitative Conditions and In- and Out-Patient Categorization

We should like to turn now to some of the major process studies of the present research effort. The basic analyses were 2 X 2 factorial analyses of variance for unequal **N**'s using the unweighted means method on the transformed data *(Winer, 1962).* Helpers were categorized as high- or low-functioning, and helpees were categorized as students seen at university counseling centers or hospitalized schizophrenic patients. The students had not been formally diagnosed, but our experience with such settings and our informal diagnostic judgements, made as we listened to the tape recordings, suggested that the students ranged from minimally disturbed to openly psychotic individuals, with the majority being mildly to moderately disturbed and probably best classified as neurotic.

Seven separate analyses were computed for **Experiential, Didactic, Strength, Weakness,** $S - W$ X **10, Action,** and total number of confrontations. Table 8 indicates the confrontation frequencies for both helpers and helpee categorizations. It can be seen that **Strength** and **Weakness** confrontations were used quite infrequently by low- and high-functioning helpers respectively, and both confrontations were distributed differently, relative to each other among the two groups of helpers. Consequently, it was decided to combine these confrontations by: $S - W$ X **10** in order to increase the size of the cell entries and perhaps give a better picture of the way in which these confrontations were used by the two groups of helpers.

Table 8
Confrontation Frequencies for High- and Low-Functioning Helpers with Students and Patients

	High-Functioning Helpers		Low-Functioning Helpers	
	Students (N = 6)	Patients (N = 7)	Students (N = 13)	Patients (N = 19)
Experiential	37	28	15	22
Didactic	13	11	6	6
Strength	6	2	2	1
Weakness	2	0	8	25
(S - W) x 10*	64	72	124	166
Action	5	1	8	3
Total	64	42	39	57

*This score is not a frequency count. If there were no **Strength** or **Weakness** confrontations, the score was computed by N x 10. If the number of **Strength** confrontations was greater than the number of **Weakness** confrontations, the score was that much greater than N x 10 and that much less than N x 10 if there were more **Weakness** than **Strength** confrontations.

Analyses indicated that the helper facilitative conditions had a significant main effect on Experiential-$F = 20.846$, $p<.0001$, Didactic - $F = 12.946$, $p<.001$, Strength-$F = 9.615$, $p<.01$, Weakness-$F = 3.924$, $p<.05$, S - W X 10 $F = 7.394$, $p<.01$, and total number of confrontations $F = 19.717$, $p<.001$. High-and-low functioning helpers did not differ significantly on the number of **Action** confrontations. *High-functioning helpers offered significantly more of each type of confrontation except that low-functioning helpers offered significantly more Weakness confrontations.*

The analyses also indicated that helpee categorization had a significant main effect on Strength-$F = 3.549$, $p<.07$ and S - W X 10 confrontations $F = 3.276$, $p<.08$. None of the interaction effects reached the .05 level of significance although the interaction effect for **Strength** and total number of confrontations approached significance $F = 3.486$, $p<.07$, and $F = 3.671$, $p<.06$, respectively.

To summarize the helper main effects, the high-functioning helpers offered significanly more **Experiential, Didactic, Strength,** and total number of confrontations than low-functioning helpers. Low-functioning helpers offered significantly more **Weakness** confrontations, but the number of **Action** confrontations did not differentiate between the two groups of helpers. The low-functioning helpers are willing to encourage action even though they do not understand the patient. Thus, with the exception of **Action** confrontations, a significant relationship between number and type of confrontation and the categorization of helpers as high-and low-functioning on the basis of mean levels of Empathy, Positive Regard, Genuineness, and Concreteness was established. Moreover, the differences were in the directions which had been expected from our conceptualization of the different kinds of confrontations. Finally, it should be noted that the relationship between confrontation and the facilitative conditions was demonstrated using both a correlation and analysis of variance model. This is a most important finding and lends further justification both for the assertion that helpers are not uniform and that categorization on the basis of the mean Facilitative Index is one effective way of differentiating helpers.

Helpee categorization had a significant main effect only on the number of **Action** confrontations although there was a trend toward a significant helpee main effect on both **Strength** and *S - W* **X 10** confrontations. As far as **Action** confrontations were concerned, it was clear that this was purely a helpee effect in a statistical sense since neither a significant helper nor interaction effect was generated. It can be seen from Table 8 that students equally received a relatively greater number of **Action** confrontations from both high- and low-functioning helpers.

Results by Confrontation Category

Experiential Confrontation

We should like to return to a more detailed account of the 2 X 2 factorial analyses of variance for each confrontation category. High-functioning helpers offered significantly more **Experiential** confrontations than low-functioning helpers when students and hospitalized patients were grouped together. In addition, the high-functioning helpers offered significantly more **Experiential** confrontations separately to students $t = 2.395, p<.05$ and patients $t = 3.164, p<.01$. However, neither high-nor low-functioning helpers offered **Experiential** confrontations differentially to students as opposed to patients. It must be pointed out, however, that the experiential confrontations offered by the highs were significantly more accurate, *used by the patients,* than those offered by the lows.

Didactic Confrontation

High-functioning helpers offered significantly more

41

Didactic confrontations than low-functioning helpers. This difference was due primarily to high-functioning helpers offering significantly more **Didactic** confrontation than low-functioning helpers to students $t = 2.382$, $p<.05$. High-and low-functioning helpers did not differ significantly when they saw hospitalized patients though there was a trend toward significance $t = 2.013$, $p<.10$, nor did either high-or low-functioning helpers offer **Didactic** confrontations differentially to students in contrast to patients.

Action Confrontation

The analysis of **Action** confrontations generated neither a significant helper main effect nor a significant interaction effect. However, students received significantly more **Action** confrontations than patients. From a statistical point of view, this was purely a helpee effect since neither helper nor interaction effects were significant. However, consideration of **Action** confrontations raises an important statistical issue.

Our data, and all helping data which are not the result of experimental manipulation, basically conform to a correlational and not an analysis of variance model. We can describe the data as related, but we cannot speak of cause and effect relationships. For this reason, Cohen *(1968)* has argued *against* the use of analyses of variance for such data and *for* the use of multiple regression methods instead. Although we are in substantial agreement with Cohen's position, analyses of variance and multiple regression analysis allow an examination of interaction effects. Often, from a clinician's viewpoint, these effects are most intriguing. Clearly, they are for us.

The significant helpee main effect on the number of **Action** confrontations points up a major difficulty in using the analysis of variance model. In the great majority of helping research, we cannot specify a cause—effect relationship. In this case, we cannot say if students *elicited* significantly more **Action** confrontations or if both high- and low-functioning helpers *chose* to offer more **Action** confrontations to students than to patients. In either case, it seems reasonable that students should receive more exhortations to act, since they certainly have more opportunities to act on their significant others than do hospitalized schizophrenics. Nevertheless, while statistically we can speak of a helpee main effect, obviously this has little clinical meaning. As noted earlier the action confrontations of the lows were stereotyped and offered indiscriminately.

Total Confrontations

High-functioning helpers offered significantly more total number of confrontations than low-functioning helpers. This was true when they saw either students $t = 2.744, p<.01,$ or patients $t = 2.234, p<.05.$ The interaction effect approached significance because high-functioning helpers tended to offer relatively more total confrontations to students as compared to patients, whereas low-functioning helpers offered approximately the same number to each. Again, although a cause-effect relationship cannot be demonstrated, it seems reasonable that students who, on the average were healthier, should receive more confrontations than patients at least within the first interview. Perhaps high-functioning helpers responded to this helpee difference while low-functioning helpers did not. The high-functioning helpers justly expected more from healthier patients.

Strength and Weakness Confrontations

Use of **Weakness** confrontations when viewed alone were fairly straightforward, but when considered in conjunction with **Strength** confrontations, appeared to be more complex. Low-functioning helpers offered significantly more **Weakness** confrontations than high-functioning helpers. The two groups of helpers did not differ significantly in confronting either students or helpees separately nor did either group of helpers offer **Weakness** confrontations differentially to students in

43

contrast to patients.

The high-functioning helpers offered a significantly greater number of confrontations to students $t = 2.160,$ $p<.05.$ In addition, both the helpee main effect and interaction effect tended toward significance. Students received more **Strength** confrontations from *both* high-and low-functioning helpers; however, high-functioning helpers offered more **Strength** confrontations to their patients than low-functioning helpers did to either students or patients In other words, although both groups of helpers confronted students more than patients on **Strengths,** high-functioning helpers offered more **Strength** confrontations to both helpee groups than low-functioning helpers did to *either* helpee group. The nearly significant helpee effect, therefore, was due to student's receiving more **Strength** confrontations from *both* high-and low-functioning helpers. The nearly significant interaction effect was due to the fact that the high-functioning helpers offered a proportionately greater number of **Strength** confrontations than the low-functioning helpers to students rather than patients.

Analysis of S - W **X 10**, where the number of **Strength** and **Weakness** confrontations were considered in relation to each other, indicated that high-functioning helpers offered significantly more **Strength** relative to **Weakness** confrontations to both students and patients than did the low-functioning helpers. For each helpee category, the difference between helpers tended toward significance *students: t = 1.856, p <.10; and patients: t = 1.951, p <.10.* In addition, since students received more **Strength** relative to **Weakness** confrontations than patients, the helpee main effect approached significance.

Taken together, the offerings of **Strength, Weakness,** and S - W **X 10** confrontations led us to some interesting clinical hypotheses. First, low-functioning helpers offered significantly more **Weakness** confrontations and **Weakness** relative to **Strength** confrontations to both students and patients than high-functioning helpers. Even more important, low-functioning helpers offered somewhat more **Weakness** and **Weakness** relative to **Strength** confrontations to patients as opposed to students whereas high-functioning helpers did the opposite: We referred to evidence which indicated that helpers who function at below minimally facilitative conditions produce either no change or helpee deterioration *(Carkhuff, 1969; Carkhuff and Berenson, 1967; Truax and Carkhuff, 1967).* Although it seems completely reasonable that helpers who offer low levels of Empathy, Positive Regard, Genuineness, and Concreteness would not elicit helpee improvement, it does not necessarily follow that they should produce helpee deterioration. After all, it seems fair to assume that helpees had been receiving low levels of the same or similar conditions in various forms from their significant others for quite some time or they probably would not be in helping. Of course, it might be argued that receiving low levels from helpers is relatively more destructive since helpees had expected more from them. This argument does not impress us since it is our experience that helpees, at least initially, do not expect any better treatment from helpers than they have received from their significant others. Indeed, the turning point in effective helping probably occurs when the helpee realizes he is being treated differently and that he can also get his significant others to treat him differently. Our data on the use of **Strength** and **Weakness** confrontations in the first helping interview provide clear instances of helper *behavior* which may lead to helpee deterioration. Low-functioning helpers focused on helpee disordered behavior significantly more often than high-functioning helpers and, furthermore, focused on the disordered behavior of those perhaps least able to profit from it — hospitalized schizophrenics — even more than they focused on students' disordered behavior. It is not at all unreasonable to hypothesize that such helper behavior not only disrupts the helpee's status quo *(however poor that may be),* but disrupts the helpee in the direction of focusing perhaps more intensively than ever on his disordered behavior with accompanying deteriorative results. The weakness was frequently created, and the low-functioning helper offered no way out.

In this connection, a word should be said about the way high-functioning helpers used **Strength** confrontations. From our discussion of the low-functioning helpers' use of **Weakness** confrontations, it might be expected that high-functioning helpers would have used more **Strength** confrontations with patients than with students. Our data indicated that this was not the case. Although high-functioning helpers offered more **Strength** and **Strength** relative to **Weakness** confrontations to both students and patients than low-functioning helpers did to either helpee group, high-functioning helpers tended to offer more **Strength** and **Strength** relative **Weakness** confrontations to students than to patients. The expectation here is that there are, in fact, more strengths to respond to in an out-patient and that the high functioning helper could more accurately identify strengths. In addition, by focusing on strength with the healthier patient the helpers increase the chances for an early patient success experience. This, in turn, facilitates the altering of the maladaptive behaviors. The patient in the hospital may first want to know if the helper can accurately discriminate his level of disfunction. In any case, it should be remembered that although high functioning helpers offered more **Strength** and **Strength** relative to **Weakness** confrontations to students, they also offered more to patients than did the low-functioning helpers who, conversely, focused on **Weakness** more than **Strength**.

Mention should be made of our discussion of the relative numbers of **Strength** and **Weakness** confrontations offered by these high-and low-functioning helpers to students and patients when such relative offerings were not significantly different. In another study dealing with helpee outcome for a different sample of helpers, it was found that **Strength, Weakness,** and the number of **Strength** plus **Action** confrontations were related to helpee outcome *(Mitchell and Wargo, 1969)*.

Thus, although a relatively small number of **Strength** and **Weakness** confrontations occurred within the first interview for these 56 helpers, these confrontations seem to take on great importance over the course of helping.

Presence and Type of Confrontation as a Function of Helper Facilitative Conditions and Helpee Level of Self-Exploration

Helpees were also categorized as high and low self-exploring on the basis of depth of self-exploration in Interpersonal Processes (Carkhuff, 1964). Essentially, the scale attempts to measure the degree to which the helpee discusses personally relevant, and often painful, material about himself in an active and spontaneous manner. Like the scales used to measure helpers levels of Empathy, Positive Regard, Genuineness, and Concreteness, Depth of Self-Exploration (EX) was derived from a similar scale originally reported by Carkhuff *(1969)*. The present scale has five levels similar to the scales employed to measure the other dimensions. In addition, at the highest levels emphasis continues to be on helpee personally relevant material in *interpersonal* situations. The earlier scales tended toward rating as high self-exploration helpee internal monologues which often had no referent other than the helpee and which thus, often tended to be "autistic".

A third pair of independent raters listened to three-minute segments from the beginning, middle, and end of each helping hour and an EX score was assigned to each helpee based on the mean score of the two raters. Pearson rate-rerate reliabilities for the two raters were .90 and .95. The intercorrelations between the raters was .76.

The mean EX score for all 56 helpees was used to categorize the helpees into high and low self-exploring groups. Those helpees with a mean of 2.02 and above were classified as high self-explorers and those helpees with a mean E score below 2.02 were termed low self-explorers. Means for the high and low EX helpees were 2.73 and 1.66, respectively.

Table 9 indicates the distributions of the number and types of confrontation as a function of both helper Facilitative Index and helpee EX. An important finding was that, when helpees were categorized as high and low self-explorers on the basis of the mean EX score for all 56 helpers, only three of the thirteen helpees seen by the high functioning helpers engaged in relatively low self-exploration. On the other hand, when those low-functioning helpers who confronted their helpees at least once were considered, 24 of their 32 helpees were classified as low self-explorers. Clearly, helpees of helpers who offered significantly higher levels of Empathy, Positive Regard, Genuineness and Concreteness explored themselves more deeply than helpees of helpers who offered significantly lower conditions. As Carkhuff *(1969)* reports, helpees' exploration is a precondition for understanding, and understanding, *by helpee and helper,* is a precondition for helper-offered initiative conditions such as confrontation. The helpees of low-functioning helpers never, or rarely, engage in deep exploration of personally relevant material, hence subsequent helper confrontations are inaccurate and absurd.

A comprehensive analysis of variance was not possible because of the degree to which the scores were unequal and the small N in many of the cells of the high helper group. Consequently, the data were analyzed separately for high- and low-functioning helpers. The chi-square computed on the confrontation data generated by the high-functioning helpers was not significant, *using Yate's correction.* Thus, high-functioning helpers did not differentially confront helpees who, during the initial interview, respond at relatively high and low levels of self-exploration.

Table 9

Frequency and Type of Confrontation as a Function of Helper Facilitative Index and Helpee Depth of Self-Exploration

Confrontation	High-Functioning Helpers		Low-Functioning Helpers	
	High EX Helpees (N = 10)	Low EX Helpees (N = 3)	High EX Helpees (N = 8)	Low EX Helpees (N = 24)
Experiential	50	15	6	31
Didactic	17	7	4	8
Strength	7	1	0	3
Weakness	1	1	7	25
Action	3	3	1	10
Total	78	27	18	78
(S - W) X 10	106	30	73	216

Table 10

Analysis of Variance for Low-Level Helpers, Level of Patient Self-Exploration, and Frequency and Type of Confrontation

Source	df	SS	MS	F
Level of Self-Exploration	1	3.260	3.260	
Type of Confrontation	3	156.144	52.048	12.12*
Level of Self-Exploration X Type of Confrontation	3	3.459	1.153	
Error Within	164	704.459	4.295	
Total	171	867.322		

Note. — Frequency of the **Strength** confrontation was so small: *two with low self-exploring patients and zero with high self-exploring patients,* that this type of confrontation was combined with weakness for this analysis; scores were computed by multiplying the average level of self-exploration by the frequency for each type of confrontation for each low helper-helpee pair.

*$p < .001$

Table 10 reflects the analysis of variance for low-functioning helpers, depth of helpee self-exploration, and frequency and type of confrontation.

The analysis of variance on the data generated by the 43 low-functioning helpers suggested several important findings. High and low levels of self-exploration helpee groups did not yield a significant effect, indicating that helpee depth of self-exploration did not determine differential confrontation by low-functioning helpers largely because it is dependent upon level of helper-offered conditions. However, the low-functioning helper had a much greater proportion of low self-exploring patients than did the high-functioning helpers: *34.9 for the low helpers and 3.10 for the high helpers.* Thus, helpees of high-functioning helpers generated significantly deeper levels of self-exploration than did helpees of low-functioning helpers.

Type of confrontation yielded a significant effect $p < .001$, suggesting that low-functioning helpers employ types of confrontation differentially. For example, in no instance did the low-functioning helper use a **Strength** confrontation with the high self-exploring helpees, and on only two instances did he employ this type of confrontation when seeing low self-exploring helpees. The 43 low-functioning helpers did employ the **Weakness** confrontation seven times with high self-exploring helpees and twenty-five times with low self-exploring helpees. The low-functioning helper seems always to be searching out vulnerabilities. *The 13 high helpers employed the* **Strength** *confrontation seven times and* **Weakness** *once, each with high and low self-exploring helpees.* A more dramatic comparison is evident in the differential use of the Experiential type of confrontation by high-and low-functioning helpers. The 13 high helpers employed **Experiential** confrontation 65 times, while the 43 low-functioning helpers employed it only 38 times. The low-functioning helper was as likely to confront a patient with his weaknesses as was the high-functioning helper to employ **Experiential** confrontation. This suggests the lows are really not in tune with the helpees' experiences.

The interaction between the level of helpee self-exploration and type of confrontation did not yield a significant effect. It appears that during the first interview, neither the high nor the low helper was significantly influenced by the level of patient self-exploration. The high helper frequently shared his experience and attended to helpee assets, while the low-functioning helper appeared to focus on exposure of helpee pathology. Consequently, unlike the student, patient categorization, high and low self-exploring helpees had little or no effect on helper-initiated confrontation within the

51

first helping interview. As mentioned earlier, helpee level of self-exploration is dependent upon level of helper-offered conditions. Hence, most of the helpees of the highs explored material at deeper levels than did the helpees of the lows. Differential use of confrontation in terms of level of helpee self-exploration for highs and lows yields insignificance.

4

Confrontation

For those helpers who possess a very limited repertoire of responses to helpee statements, the major
aspects or dimensions of helping are accepted as being
mutually exclusive. That is, if they attempt to be warm
and understanding, they make no attempt to give the
process direction. In addition, these helpers invariably
function low on all critical dimensions *(Carkhuff, 1969)*.
Beyond the narrow limitations of their verbal, emotional and physical resources, the low-level functioning
helper, trainer, parent or teacher experiences himself or
herself caught up in the choice between being tender,
gentle, warm, and unconditionally regarding or being
assertive, directionful, confronting, immediate and
highly conditional in regard for the helpee. Whatever
their final or even momentary choice, they function
below minimally facilitative levels *(Alexik and Carkhuff,
1967; Anthony and Carkhuff, 1969; Berstein and
Carkhuff, 1969; Cannon and Carkhuff, 1969; Pierce,
Carkhuff and Berenson, 1967; Bierman, 1968; Frankel,
1968; Berenson and Mitchell, 1968; Kratochvil, Carkhuff
and Berenson, 1969; Aspy, 1967; Aspy and Hadlock,
1967)*.

The most effective helpers, however, put these polar
dimensions together and in a sequence that is both
interrelated and systematic. That is, they demonstrate a
large repertoire of responsive and initiative responses.
Further, they are initially more responsive and later in
the helping process both responsive and action oriented.
Those helpers who offer the highest levels of responsive
dimensions also provide the highest levels of the action-
oriented dimensions *(Berenson and Mitchell, 1968;
Berenson, Mitchell and Moravec, 1968; Carkhuff, 1970;
Mitchell, 1971)*.

More specifically, studies *(Carkhuff and Berenson,
1967; Piaget, Berenson and Carkhuff, 1967; Truax and
Carkhuff, 1967; Mitchell, Mitchell and Berenson, 1970)*
have demonstrated the differential effect of level of
helper functioning on helpee depth of self-exploration.
Other research *(Alexik and Carkhuff, 1967; Carkhuff*

and Alexik, 1967; Friel, Kratochvil and Carkhuff, 1969; and Holder, Carkhuff and Berenson, 1967) has further demonstrated the effects of the manipulation of helpee depth of self-exploration upon high and low-functioning helpers. Helpers functioning at high levels tended to perform independently of the helpee's manipulation with the highest level helper offering even higher levels at the point of a decrease in the helpee's depth of self-exploration. All of the low-level functioning helpers dropped still lower in their levels of functioning during the same kind of manipulation period and none returned to their initial relatively higher, but low levels of performance. That is, at any crisis point the helper who on the average offers low levels of such dimensions as, empathic understanding, respect, and genuineness, retreats from relevant and personal discourse. In contrast, the best and most effective helpers tend to move to even higher levels following some crisis in the helping situation.

It was felt that the effective helpers provided something more to their helpees than a responsive set, not only at crises points, but in general throughout their helping on therapeutic efforts. That is, a responsive set does not provide direction and the experience of directly acting on the world. Even the highest level reflections of deep feelings do not culminate in an act by either helper or helpee.

Additional studies *(Berenson and Mitchell, 1968; Berenson, Mitchell and Laney, 1968; Berenson, Mitchell and Moravec, 1968; Mitchell, 1967; Mitchell and Mitchell, 1967; Mitchell, Mitchell and Berenson, 1970)* reported significant relationships among level of helper functioning on dimensions such as Empathic Understanding, Respect, Concreteness and Genuineness with seemingly more assertive dimensions such as Immediacy, Reference to Significant Others, and the type and frequency of helper-initiated confrontations.

The study reported in some detail in this chapter systematically examined the interrelationships among

54

helper-offered levels of Empathy, Regard or Respect, Genuineness, Concreteness, Helpee Self-Exploration, Immediacy, Reference to Significant Others and frequency of helper Confrontation *(Carkhuff, 1969)*. Basically, in this study we wished to explore the possibility that the interpersonal processes offered by helpers functioning at high and low levels are not only functionally different but also structurally different. Beyond this we hoped to learn more about the presence and function of assertive helper behaviors.

Method

Forty-five first interviews were assessed for level of helper functioning by objective tape ratings of helper-offered conditions of the core conditions: Empathy, E; Regard, R; Genuineness, G; and Concreteness, C; as well as the process variables: Immediacy of Relationship, IRS; Reference to Significant Others, SO; and Frequency of Confrontation, C. Raters were two helpers with nine and four years of experience. The helpers represented a wide sample of experience ranging from advanced level graduate students in clinical and counseling psychology to helpers with more than 18 years of experience who were employed in an out-patient clinic and college counseling centers. Helpees ranged from minimally disturbed college students to hospitalized schizophrenics. It is important to note, however, that Berenson, Mitchell and Laney *(1968)* did not find a significant interaction between level of helper functioning and type of helpee.

Helpers were classified as functioning at high or low levels based on average tape ratings of the four core conditions, *E; R; G; C.* Those helpers functioning on the average above 2.5 (on 5—point scales) were categorized as high-level, and those functioning below 2.5 were categorized as low-level. The mean level of performance for the low-level helpers was 1.60, and for the high-level helpers, 3.30. The scales employed to determine the level of helper-offered *E, R, G, C* have been extensively described elsewhere *(Carkhuff and Berenson, 1967; Carkhuff, 1969).*

The variables IRS and SO were rated using 6 and 15 point scales respectively. Frequency of Confrontation was rated as the summation of the five possible types of confrontation suggested by Berenson, Mitchell, and Laney (1968).

All ratings were taken during two identified periods:

1. Base rate period — which was four three minute excerpts taken randomly from each interview;
2. Post confrontation period — all helper confrontations throughout each interview were identified, and the variable E, R, G, IRS, SO were rated during the three-minute period following each identified helper confrontation.

Raw scores for all seven process variables and helpee self-exploration *(EX* for the high *N = 13,* and low *N = 32* helpers) for both the base rate and post-confrontation periods were submitted to Principle Component analysis *(Lohnes, 1966).* The factor structure was selected on the basis that all factors must yield eight values 1.00 *(Kaiser, 1960).* Further, an additional factor was submitted to rotation for each group so that all test variables may be represented on all factors. Beyond this, only factor pattern scores exceeding .45 are reported as significant. This cut-off follows the suggestion of Lohnes *(1966)* and is raised to its present level in order to partially control for excessive variability of factor loadings due to relatively small samples.

Discussion of Results

Differences among the factor patterns for the high, low and combined groups were evident in the results of the component analysis. The differences occurred for the interrelationships of all the variables based on ratings for base rate and post confrontation.

TABLE 11
Total Group Factor Patterns,
Varimax Rotation of Three Factor Scheme,
for Base Rate and Post Confrontation Factors
greater than .45

Variable	Symbol	Base Rate Factors			Post Confrontation Factors		
		I	II	III	I	II	III
Frequency of Confrontation	#c		.89		.72		
Empathy	E	.88			.77	.58	
Regard	R	.82	.52		.79	.56	
Genuineness	G	.79	.55		.85	.46	
Concreteness	C	.88			.81	.51	
Client Self-Exploration	Dx	.89				.91	
Immediacy	IRS		.66	.59	.88		
Significant Other Reference	SOS			.97			.96
Proportion of Variance Extracted		.50	.26	.16	.52	.26	.13

TABLE 12
Varimax Rotation of Two Low-Functioning Helper Sub Samples n=13 for Base Rate Factors *greater than .45*

Variable	Symbol	Factor I Group		Factor II Group		Factor III Group	
		1	2	1	2	1	2
Frequency of Confrontation	#C			.79	.91		
Empathy	E	.93	.96				
Regard	R	.94	.88				
Genuineness	G	.93	.87				
Concreteness	C	.90	.88				
Client Self-Exploration	Dx		.83	.83			
Immediacy	IRS				.57	.91	.75
Significant Other Reference	SOS					.91	.89
Proportion of Variance Extracted		.45	.50	.18	.17	.23	.20

It appeared that ignoring helper level of functioning by pooling leads to misrepresenting both groups, high and low — *Table 11.* That is, the post-confrontation pattern for the total group does not characterize either of the other groups examined separately. The impact of the high-level helpers is neutralized or moderated when their ratings were pooled with ratings of the low-level helpers. Differential results, when they do occur, are a result of the ratings of high-level helpers only. Studies reporting on the effectiveness of helping strongly support this finding *(Bergin, 1963; Betz, 1963; Truax and Carkhuff, 1967; Whitehorn, 1964; Carkhuff and Berenson, 1967).* A constantly larger number of low-level helpers constantly wash out the constructive impact of high-level helpers.

Other studies *(Antonozzio and Kratochvil, 1968; Greenbaum, 1968; Greenberg, 1968; Carkhuff, 1970)* suggest that helpers providing given levels of responsive dimensions also provide comparable levels of other process dimensions. Most important, however, was the finding that the low-level helper never reaches the high-level helper's ratings on any of the variables. Predictions of outcome based on the pooled ratings of high and low-functioning helpers can only replicate the finding that helping on the average has the same mean effect as no help *(Eysenck, 1952; Levitt, 1954).*

Classification of process variables:
In order to facilitate the task of interpreting complex factor patterns, the variables were grouped as follows:

Helper-Responsive Variables

Empathic Understanding
Respect

Helper-Initiative Variables

Immediacy Interpretations
Number of Confrontations
Reference to Significant Others

Genuineness
Concreteness

59

Therapist or helper-responsive conditions include empathic understanding and respect or positive regard. The basic intent of these dimensions is to communicate to the patient or helpee that the helper understands the feeling and content of what the helpee is, or was, experiencing without imposing interpretations or direction.

Genuineness and Concreteness appear to be multi-dimensional. In part, they are responsive when the helper shares his experience or offers a specific reflection of information. They are initiative in situations where the helper, out of his own needs or perspective, shares his full experience or operates to refocus the direction of the interaction.

Immediacy and number of confrontations are clearly initiative variables. At its highest level, Reference to Significant Others is an initiative variable and merges with Immediacy Interpretations.

TABLE 13
High and Low-Functioning Helper Factor Patterns Varimax Rotation,
3-Factor Schemes and Variables
Means, for Base Rate Factors *greater than .45*

Variable Symbol	Variable Mean by Helper Groups		Factor Patterns by Helper Groups					
			I		II		III	
	High	Low	High	Low	High	Low	High	Low
#C	8.08	3.00	.84					.89
E	3.19	1.64	.56	.91	.79			
R	3.32	1.62	.96	.92				
G	3.51	1.56	.89	.93				
C	3.07	1.73		.92	.55	.70		
D_χ	2.66	1.90		.62	.89			.46
IRS	3.78	2.54	.85			.80		
SOS	6.02	4.48				.93	.88	
Proportion of Variance Extracted			.47	.53	.22	.18	.17	.13

60

TABLE 14
High and Low-Functioning Helpers Factor Patterns Varimax Rotation, 3 Factor Schemes and Variable Means
For Post-Confrontation Factors *greater than .45*

Variable Symbol	Variable Mean by Helper Group		Factor Patterns by Helper Group					
			I		II		III	
	High	Low	High	Low	High	Low	High	Low
#C	8.08	3.00		.60	.88			
E	3.30	1.75	.94	.90				
R	3.21	1.67	.95	.91				
G	3.24	1.71	.91	.94				
C	2.99	1.85	.85	.91				
D_X	2.49	1.79					.94	.89
IRS	4.26	2.65	.49	.80	.65			
SOS	6.90	4.67			.83	.99		
Proportion of Variance Extracted			.51	.59	.25	.12	.14	.16

Low-Functioning Helpers

It is important to keep in mind that low-level helpers functioned poorly on both sets of variables and this finding is consistent with the results or studies cited earlier in this chapter. This is also congruent with the moderator variable concept in that, I, C, SO, are based upon an entirely different theoretical framework than were the other variables included in the analysis. There is no doubt that helper level of functioning is an appropriate predictive measure as well as a vehicle for helping us understand the successes and failures of our helping efforts. It is also obvious that this dichotomy — *high-low* — is functional and has profound implications for selection and training *(Carkhuff, 1970).*

In summary, the low-level helper *for base rate and post-confrontation* independent of the differential factor structure, provides a helping encounter that is:

1. Subtractive in terms of empathic understanding, respect, genuineness and concreteness.

2. Characterized by low levels of helpee self-exploration.

3. Preoccupied with references to non-significant others.

4. Lacking in confrontation.

Proponents of all orientations and schools of therapy would agree that this sort of process will and does result in deleterious impact upon the life of the helpee; yet it describes what is typically passed off as helping *(Berenson and Carkhuff, 1967; Carkhuff and Berenson, 1967).*

Base Rate for Low-Functioning Helpers

(see Table XIII)

Factor I. *53% variance* — This factor, *E; R; G; C; moderate EX,* reflects a low-level helper responsive process devoid of accuracy, depth, relevant material, and one likely to be experienced by the helpee as an encounter that leaves him with less than he had when he started. It leaves the helpee with just another among many experiences that have at best confirmed his impotence and, at worst, confirmed his destructive orientation toward himself, others, and life itself.

Factor II. *18% variance* — The mean levels of the variables in this factor, *I and SO,* suggest a process made up of remote and relatively insignificant issues. Although this factor is composed of initiative variables, it cannot be seen as functionally initiative or assertive in the usual sense. It is active in the sense that the helper does whatever he can to avoid salient, relevant relationships and the full meaning and impact of the immediate situation.

Factor III. *13% variance* — This factor, *CDX,* appears to be a bipolar factor. Although an inverse relationship exists between the number of confrontations and depth of helpee self-exploration for low-level functioning helpers, it is critical to keep in mind that low levels of self-exploration are invariably accompanied by low levels of helper E, G, C, and R. Infrequent confrontations, $C = 3$, $DX = 1.9$, occur in the absence of high levels of the Responsive dimensions, and are likely to additionally contribute to the helpee's offerings of personally irrelevant material.

It would seem then, that high levels of helpee self-exploration brought about by high levels of helper-offered responsive dimensions is a usual prerequisite to constructive use of confrontation. The negative response

63

to low levels of the Responsive dimensions appear to be compounded by providing the helpee with infrequent confrontations geared most often by the low-level functioning helper to focus on helpee weaknesses.

Thus, the combination of low levels of E, R, G, C, as well as infrequent confrontations, serves the inadequate helper by keeping the material offered by the helpee shallow and distant — suggesting that he, *the inadequate helper,* knows full well that he can only provide the apparency of helping. In essence, then, his inability to understand, to respect his helpee and to provide vivid moments of truth is, for the ineffectual helper, a defense mechanism. Further, his helpee is conditioned not to expect to be confronted, and when it does occur, it becomes a signal to the helpee that his explorations may be approaching immediate relevance and personal intensity. The helpee is negatively reinforced whenever he begins not to appear needy or sick.

Post-Confrontation Factors for Low-Functioning Helpers

(see Table XIV)

Throughout the discussion of the post-confrontation factors for low-level functioning helpers, it is important to keep in mind that although there are slight factor pattern changes the average levels of all variables remain low.

Factor I. *59% variance* — Although this factor is made up of both helper responsive, *E; R; G; C,* and initiative dimensions, *I and #C,* the low mean scores on all of them remind us that this apparent combination probably does not functionally make a difference. All variables are operating to subtract from the helpee's experience as well as any possibility of constructive direction.

When we compare this factor with Factor I of the base rate for low-functioning helpers, we find that **EX** dropped out and that **#C** and *I* now lead significantly.

During the post-confrontation period, the low-level helper attempts to provide an impotent apparency of immediacy and genuineness as well as his continued low levels of understanding and regard. All dimensions are provided independent of the helpee, his problem, his feelings and his attempts to tell the helper that the process and the helper are not, in fact, helping.

Beyond this, it is obvious that these helpers do not or are unable to, follow their own initiated confrontations with even minimally facilitative levels of responsiveness or immediacy. It is as if they are functioning without the slightest awareness of what is happening in the helpee, the situation, or themselves.

During the post-confrontation period, helpee **EX** *Factor III, 16% variance* and **SO** *Factor II, 12% variance* become independent factors. The **EX** factor is obviously appropriate for the data reflecting the performance of high-level helpers. In this instance for the low-level helpers this factor must, as is the case with other factors, be understood in terms of low scores throughout the ratings. Once again, the helping process including the contributions of the helpee, for base rate and post-confrontation periods, is virtually independent of the verbal, emotional, and behavioral input of the helpee.

Although the low-functioning helper does initiate, he does so to relate the process to only the most superficial levels of helpee self-exploration. Briefly, these helpers do what they can to appear to be involved, but they actually function to avoid involvement and personal responsibility. That is, they appear to know the process will fail before they start it and set processes in motion so that the helpee will appear to be responsible for the failure. This is most vividly accomplished by doing things that result in the helpee appearing to be irrational and the helper an apparently objective prober of pathology. More specifically, these helpers:

1. Ask a large number of questions that do

not elicit spontaneous and personally relevant material, but do give the impression that the helper is doing what he should be doing.

2. Avoid attending to the immediate, and focus on remote happenings so that they appear to be systematic collectors of data that explain the helpee's distress.

3. Do not allow the process to focus on highly significant others so that the process stays away from discussions involving the helper.

4. Do not communicate to experts that they understand or respect the helpee; claiming that the whole thing is too complex, or that an outsider could never really appreciate the whole thing and that after all there are no objective means for evaluating.

5. Are not willing or able to share their personal experience of the helpee in terms personally relevant for the helpee, a step resulting in additional frustration for the helpee.

There are other diversionary and often cruel tactics employed by the inadequate helper. A crucial point to make, however obvious, is that such conditions can only bring about helpee behavior that can be interpreted as pathological as long as the focus is on the helpee. Once we attend to the interdependent interaction between helper and helpee behaviors, it is clear that this kind of helper does not:

1. Provide a facilitative model *(Bandura,*

1965; Carkhuff, 1970).

2. Become a potent and constructive rein-forcer *(Truax and Carkhuff, 1965; Cark-huff, 1970).*

3. Allow helpee self-exploration of imme-diately relevant material *(Carkhuff and Berenson, 1967; Carkhuff, 1970).*

4. Provide the preconditions and follow-through necessary for understanding and consequent constructive action in life *(Carkhuff, 1970).*

High-Functioning Helpers

It is obvious that high-functioning helpers provide a very different experience than do low-functioning helpers. These differences are clearly evident in average levels of helping conditions offered the helpee for both base rate and post-confrontation. These differences are also in evidence in the composition of the factors for both categories of helpers. This evidence and the studies cited earlier strongly suggest that effective and ineffec-tive helpers do not differ in degree, but may well repre-sent different populations of helpers: all helpers are not cut from the same mold. Carkhuff *(1971)* recommends that those not functioning at minimally facilitative levels *(level 3)* should be trained to do so, and those not train-able, treated as helpees. People seem to do strange things when they are asked to do things they can not do. When they accept pay to do things they can not do, they are psychopaths.

67

Base Rate for High-Functioning Helpers

When we examine the average level of functioning for the more effective helpers, it becomes quite clear they provide a very different helping encounter. It is different not only experientially but also structurally. These differences occur across all dimensions as well as base rate and post-confrontation data.

(see Table III)

Factor I. *47% variance* — This is a complex factor in that it combines both responsive *(E, R, G)* and initiative *(C, I)* dimensions. Thus, the high-level functioning helper apparently combines what appears to be mutually exclusive processes for less effective helpers. While responding fully to the helpee, this level helper can at the same time initiate confrontations based on his deep level of understanding, as well as give the entire interaction an immediate, intense focus. The effective helper is at his creative best dealing with the most personal aspects of the here and now while at the same time communicating the deepest levels of understanding and respect. In this way the helper demonstrates how full and rich a responsibly honest relationship can be, not for the benefit of the helpee alone but also for his own benefit. It is at these moments that he must struggle to comprehend a new experience. The helper understands full well that his success contributes to his own growth as well as demonstrating to his helpee that growth really is possible. The helpee has resolved himself to the certainty of deterioration in order to avoid the uncertainties of growth. The directionful behavior of the helper for his own benefit and the helpee, takes away a great deal of this uncertainty. If the helper's first demands of the helpee are things the helpee can do, the helpee can then begin to understand for the first time that meeting these demands constitutes the first steps toward growth. He is in effect creating the atmosphere within which he wishes the relationship to develop. In addition, the helper serves as an effective model: a person who can both respond and act upon his understanding. Functionally, this factor appears to be preparation for Factor II *(E, C, DX)*: The relationship of helpee self-exploration to empathic understanding and concreteness.

Factor II. *22% variance* —This factor *(E, C, DX)* seems most critical in the light of research efforts to link helpee self-exploration to levels of helper functioning *(Berenson and Carkhuff, 1967; Carkhuff and Berenson, 1967; Rogers, 1957; Truax and Carkhuff, 1967)*. Factors for the low-functioning helpers *(E, R, G, C, EX)* demonstrate that at low levels, low helpee **EX** is related to low levels of all core conditions. This factor *(E, C, EX)* demonstrates that at high levels of helper functioning, only two of the core conditions are related directly to **EX**. The other core conditions *(R, G)* apparently are more critical in establishing the type of atmosphere where deeper levels of **EX** can be expressed freely *(Carkhuff and Berenson, 1967; Carkhuff, 1970)*.

Factor III. *17% variance* — This third factor *(C, SO)* suggests a somewhat specific factor, in that it represents the helper's initiation of discussion of personally relevant, significant relationships in the helpee's life. The mean level of **SO**, *6.02,* suggests that the helper-helpee relationship has not fully reached that stage where the helper becomes the most significant other for the helpee, i.e., in a fully immediate relationship that deals extensively with the here and now.

Post-Confrontation Factors

(see Table IV)

The post-confrontation factors suggest a dual process for high-functioning helpers. Primarily *(Factor I, 51% variance, E, R, G, C, moderate IRS)*, they offer a responsive process, keenly tuned into and focusing on

69

the helpee. Secondly, *(Factor II, 25% variance, C, SO, IRS)* they follow up the initial confrontation by initiating direction based on the immediate and significant personal relationships of the helpee, independent of the helpee's **EX** *(Factor III, 14% variance, EX).*

The process suggested by these factors is a helpee-centered process, *not necessarily helpee-centered helping,* supportive and accepting in general, yet directionful, and at times independent of the helpee. It is critical to realize that even while operating independently of the helpee's **EX,** high-functioning helpers are not operating independent of the helpee as a person, *as low levels of facilitative conditions would represent,* but rather are operating in the interest of the helpee's potential, experience and value as a human being *(high levels of E, R, G, C)* by making judgements and making demands on the helpee.

Summary

Two general findings of this study are:

1. Helpers functioning at given levels on the core conditions also function at correspondingly high or low levels on the additional process variables—*IRS, SO, C.*

2. Failure to differentiate levels of helper functioning leads to misrepresentation of the helping processes as a result of combining helper sub-groups that should not be statistically or meaningfully combined.

The specific results of the component analysis suggest that the interpersonal processes offered by helpers functioning at high and low levels are both functionally and structurally different during both base rate and post confrontation periods.

This difference between high and low level functioning helpers can best be described in terms of the process by which the helper interacts with the helpee. Low-level functioning helpers appear to be operating independently of any cognitive, emotional, or experiential feedback. They are either distorting it such that it becomes incongruous to the helpee's experience, or they themselves are incapable of constructively initiating the direction of the relationship as a result of their feedback. They do not have constructive responses in their repertoire.

High-functioning helpers demonstrate that they are indeed operating during both the base rate and post-confrontation periods on the feedback they receive from the helpee. In particular, they are neither distorting the helpee's messages, nor are they utilizing these messages to confront the helpee with non-facilitative experiences. Rather, high-functioning helpers seem to be operating in a multi-aspect process whereby they act responsively to obtain feedback from the helpee. Then they initiate direction as a result of learnings from prior feedback — yet during the initiation process, they are also responsive to the immediate feedback they are getting. Thus, they establish a helpee-focused, helper-initiated facilitative process that operates in the present as a function of the feedback received from the helpee.

To the extent that high-functioning helpers become models of constructive interpersonal behavior *(Bandura, 1965; Carkhuff and Berenson, 1967; Carkhuff, 1970)* and/or potent reinforcers of behavior modification *(Carkhuff and Berenson, 1967; Truax and Carkhuff, 1967; Carkhuff, 1970)*, the differential factor structures for the base rate and post-confrontation data may well represent these emerging processes.

5

Confrontation Research

Beyond the identification of helper variables which related to effective helping, the thrust of helping research must culminate in the operationalization of these variables *(Carkhuff, 1971)*. Once this was accomplished, Carkhuff *(1969; 1971)* also developed systematic programs to train helpers to employ them effectively. Thus the effective helper, like the effective worker in any field, can be identified by the quality and quantity of his skills. The implications are interesting.

The average helper is most skillful in his efforts to share the responsibility for his failure to discharge the responsibilities for which he is being paid to discharge. He has done this in many and varied ways, most often by aligning himself with a particular "school" of helping, an incomplete technology; the inappropriate and exaggerated use of some one dimension; complex explanations of the helpee's dynamics; or most frequently a retreat to psychopathic games, constitute the tactics frequently employed by such helpers.

The identification of helping as a set of responsive and initiative helper skills accompanied by demonstrations that a wide variety of persons can learn these skills *(even professional helpers)* makes it more difficult for the helper to avoid learning these skills.

The irony is that most helpers are concerned about the implications for assuming personal responsibility for the quality of their work rather than being worried about the implication for not assuming this responsibilty. The abuse of confrontation is merely another means for ineffectuals to avoid being held responsible for their deleterious impact.

The following discussion illustrates a number of the important differences between high- and low-level functioning helpers. Beyond this, the discussion illustrates vivid constrasts in life styles:

1. Anyone who accepts personal responsibility for his life will welcome all critical opportunities for personal growth; for himself and others who rely on him for

help. Those who do not must sacrifice such opportunities and often the people they are being paid to help.

2. Anyone who accepts personal responsibility for his life takes an assertive, directionful stance toward life. Those who do not can only assume a defensive stance toward life and must choose to neutralize or destroy outright any effort to expand growth experiences.

3. Anyone who accepts personal responsibility for his life is not a victim. Those who do not can only be victims, and they know that victims and killers are one and the same.

4. Anyone who accepts personal responsibility for his life knows that once he comes to understand another person better than that person understands himself, the understanding is irrelevant unless they both act on that understanding. Those who make understanding in and of itself a goal, offer the apparency of an act.

5. Anyone who accepts personal responsibility for his life, views understanding only as a precondition to action. Those who view understanding alone as relevant, are impotent.

6. Anyone who accepts personal responsibility for his life knows that once he has acted upon his understanding, the understanding becomes irrelevant. Those who do not act upon their understanding, offer only pseudo-understanding.

7. Anyone who accepts personal responsibility for his life pays any price to increase

the quality and quantity of his skills.
Those who deny that helping skills exist
offer apparent skills.

The initiative dimensions, of which confrontation is only one, have been avoided by some because it would lead to a greater degree of personal responsibility. The initiative dimensions have been abused by most — *the professional confronters* — because they do not have skills. For them, confrontation puts the focus on others because they, themselves, cannot afford scrutiny. Confrontation employed without high-level responsive skills and skills related to other initiative dimensions, *such as immediacy interpretations, systematic problem-solving, systematic program development,* is distorted in conception and pathological in function.

The following discussion of the types of confrontation demonstrates that when employed by an effective helper, confrontation can often efficiently expand the helper's and the helpee's experience rather than merely expose helpee weaknesses. Any helper who uses confrontation to exploit helpee pathology is the real helpee.

Some Implications of Confrontations Offered by High and Low-Functioning Helpers

The following discussions based on the different types of confrontations spell out the implications of the differential level of initiative skills of high and low functioning helpers.

Experiential Confrontation

The basic finding of the research was that high-and low-functioning helpers confront their helpees very differently.

Those helpers who demonstrated low-level responsive skills also demonstrated low-level initiative skills. Those helpers who demonstrated a high-level of responsive skills, demonstrated a high-level of initiative skills. Effective helpers use skills prized by all major schools of helping.

High-level helpers used significantly more experiential confrontations than did low-level helpers. In addition, the highs employed many other types of confrontation. This difference can not be over-emphasized. Within the first fifteen minutes of the first interview, the two groups of helpers offered very different experiences: $t = 3.94$, $p<.01$. The low-functioning helpers who saw hospitalized patients employed more weakness than experiential confrontations. This is a vivid contrast, particularly in the first interview. It is a clear behavioral demonstration which not only parallels the points made in the beginning of this chapter, but also earlier research *(Carkhuff and Berenson, 1967; Carkhuff, 1969, 1970; McNair and Lorr, 1964; Orlinsky and Howard, 1967a, 1967b; Suncland and Barker, 1962; Wallach and Strupp, 1964).*

There are additional differences. With all helpee populations studied, the highs offered an increasing number of experiential confrontations over time. *That is, as they came to know more about their helpees, they pressed to know even more about them.* This not only reinforced the helpee's examination and involvement in the relationship, but communicated to him that the more his helper came to understand him, the more he demanded the relationship to be conditional and fully honest. The lows seemed to communicate, "I cannot come to know you because I must pretend not to know myself. Therefore, I can *at best* only promote a mutually self denying relationship, where I con you and you learn to con me."

Clearly, the sequence of the confrontations offered by the lows suggests a pattern of *behavior* which, in the context of less than minimally responsive conditions, could lead directly to helpee deterioration. This is a point which we shall be making throughout this chapter. The action-oriented, concrete, challenging, and behavioral nature of confrontation leads us to expect that, in the context of more or less than minimally facilitative conditions, helper-initiated confrontation may well be a specific behavior which leads *directly* to helpee improvement or deterioration.

Didactic Confrontations

In light of the research indicating that helpee expectations about helping are related to positive outcome and that such expectations can be enhanced by the helper *(Begley and Lieberman, 1970; Gladstein, 1969; Greenberg, 1969; Greenberg, Goldstein and Perry, 1970; Krause, Fitzsimmons and Wolf, 1969; and Sloane, Cristol, Pepernik and Stapes, 1970)* it is noteworthy that, overall, the highs used significantly more **Didactic** confrontations than the lows. However, it is not obvious why those high-level helpers, who saw students, but not those who saw patients, would use **Didactic** confrontations significantly more often than their low facilitative counterparts. One hypothesis is that students, being students, had more *overt* concerns than hospitalized patients about objective data, and it was the helping process itself which necessitated **Didactic** confrontations. The highs, but not the lows, responded to these concerns. In this connection, hospitalized patients, at least during the first interview, are, perhaps, not goal-oriented enough, are too passive, or experience such overriding concern with their disordered behavior that a consideration of the more objective aspects of themselves, their helper, and the helping process is not uppermost among their concerns. A number of alternative hypotheses are also plausible, however. It is clear to us from both the data and our listening to the tape recordings, that the highs are much more willing than the lows to clarify helpee misinformation so that the relationship is based on fact rather than fiction, and genuineness rather than magical thinking.

We did not see **Didactic** confrontations in the same dynamic light or as clinically powerful as the other confrontations. We believe that, over the course of helping, **Didactic** confrontations become less important to helpee improvement although they very well may be efficient during the early stages to the extent that clarification of objective test data and helper and helpee roles prepares the helpee for the helping process proper and helps cement an initially tenuous relationship. **Didactic** confrontations appear similar to other helper anticipatory responses which are related to positive outcome. Their relative *absence* in the repertoire of the low-level helpers, particularly those who saw patients, is even more intriguing than their presence. There seems to be something "anally-retentive" about a helper who refused to offer pertinent, objective information to a helpee, particularly a hospitalized patient who may be in need of such clarification, although not aware enough to ask. This reluctance may reflect an inability to offer structure, and presumably security, to the relationship, an inability that may be related to the helper's feelings of impotency; or, the relative absence of **Didactic** confrontations may be passive-aggressive in nature, reflecting a sadistic impulse to have the helpee "sweat it out". In any case, perhaps the differential use of **Didactic** confrontations, particularly in the first interview, reflects basic personality differences between high and low facilitators which will effect the relationship throughout helping. Some simply do not wish to be held responsible even for factual information.

Strength and Weakness Confrontations

The differential use of **Strength** and, particularly **Weakness** confrontations provides, for us, *the third set of findings generated by the present research effort which we regard as extremely important.* The 13 high facilitators used more than twice as many **Strength** confrontations as the 43 low facilitators, although this difference was exclusively a function of those high facilitators who had seen students. On the other hand, the low facilitators used *more than 15 times as many Weakness confrontations as the high facilitators.* In this case, the difference was due largely to the low facilitators who saw patients. It would be of the utmost importance to determine a helper's reasons for using either a **Strength** or **Weakness** confrontation, but on the basis of the present data and listening to the tape recordings, we can only speculate. By most standards, however, it seems more appropriate to confront students with their strengths than patients with their weaknesses, at least at the outset of helping.

Of greatest importance to us, despite the status of the present data, is the inescapable conclusion that in the context of high and low facilitative conditions, *Strength and, particularly, Weakness confrontations are very likely specific helper behaviors which lead directly to helpee improvement or deterioration.* Initially, Truax and Carkhuff *(1967)* suggested that, on the basis of test data as well as recidivism rates, some helpees improved while others deteriorated and they related those outcomes to helper levels of Empathy, Positive Regard, and Genuineness. Indeed, these facilitative conditions are related significantly to the number of days out of hospital 10 years after initial hospital release. Nevertheless, the *change potency* of these variables has never seemed impressive to us. Carkhuff *(1969)* later suggested another helping model which placed the facilitative conditions and such action-oriented behaviors as confrontation in a different framework. Basically, he views Empathy, Positive Regard, Genuineness, and Concreteness as interpersonal characteristics of the helper which allow the helpee to like and trust him, thereby preparing the goundwork for the helper to be helpful. *The responsive conditions allow the helper to become a change agent but they do not, themselves, effect change.*

Essentially, this is our position. The helpee is in phenomenological pain because the significant others in his life have been predominantly low level facilitators *(Ellis, 1962; Hobbs, 1962; Kell and Meuller, 1966; Mitchell, Mitchell and Berenson, 1970).* He has little reason to expect different behavior from his helper. Consequently, if his helper is a low facilitator, it merely continues the deterioration and denies the helpee a growth experience. In other words, the low facilitative helper confirms his helpee's view of himself and his significant others. If he were to deteriorate, it would probably be a continuation of a long-standing process as well as the result of less than minimally facilitative levels of Empathy, Positive Regard, Genuineness and Concreteness. If the helpee's helper were a high facilitator and nothing more — *i.e., he was not more action-oriented as well,* the helpee would feel understood and respected but, in Carkhuff's terms, his "expressed phenomenological existence" would be reinforced by challenging the helpee to examine his distortions by offering the helpee the opportunity to *experience* a potent model in helping, and by forcing the helpee to act and *to experience that action* in order to save the helping aspects of the relationship. Confrontation may give the helpee the opportunity *to experience helping himself by keeping the relationship honest, and thereby, helpful.*

To return to **Strength** and **Weakness** confrontations, it is clear that **Strength** confrontations, across helper and helpee classifications, were used least of the confrontation categories. It may be that **Strength** confrontations are not particularly appropriate during the first helping session, or that high and low helpers are similar in this regard to the extent that their training mitigates their using such confrontations more frequently. Helpers, like other people, do what they are trained to do. After listening to the tape recordings, our impression is that **Strength** confrontations might have been used more often, but that their early use presents two dangers. First, most helpees are somewhat cautious at the beginning of helping and the helper probably would be seen as a "con man" if he used too many **Strength** confrontations, or he was anxious about the helpee's maladaptive behavior, denying the helpee's phenomenological pain. Second, the orientation of the early interviews should be toward understanding the helpee *as he sees himself.* Too many **Strength** confrontations probably would be disruptive under such circumstances whether they were accurate or not. For these reasons, we would expect the number of **Strength** confrontations to increase over time in effective helping because they would become more acceptable to the helpee and because, if helping were effective, there would be more basis for using such confrontations. The evidence we have on this point is that the high facilitative professionals used significantly more **Strength** confrontations than the low facilitative professionals and that the differences, although small in absolute number, were significant in the second and third time periods. That is, they increase even during the first interview. Apparently, a relatively small number of **Strength** confrontations, in the context of high responsive conditions, appears to be optimal during the first interview. It is our suspicion, however, that another possible reason for the relatively small number of **Strength** confrontations is that helpers are taught that such behavior is "pollyannish and unsophisticated". We are trained to look for pathology, and we do so with a vengeance. An interesting study bears on this point. Dole, Nottingham and Wrightsman *(1969)* studied certain attitudes of a national sample of directors of clinical and counseling psychology, and rehabilitation counseling training programs as well as those of three of their students who were chosen at random. They found that the majority of the directors wanted their students to believe that human nature is neither favorable nor unfavorable. Furthermore, approximately half believed that people were basically neither bad or good. In contrast, the students had generally neutral but slightly favorable attitudes toward people. It seems apparent in which direction the students would change over the course of their training and, under such circumstances, it is hardly surprising that **Strength** confrontations were a relatively rare occurrence.

The use of **Weakness** confrontations in this regard is particularly important. The 13 highs used such confrontations only twice, on both occasions with students. The 32 low facilitators used more than 15 times as many, the majority of them with hospitalized patients. At first glance, such behavior might seem appropriate: helpees come to helping to talk about their problems and, ostensibly, one function of the helper is to uncover hidden problems. It should be remembered, however, that by definition a **Weakness** confrontation is a helper-initiated behavior which focuses on pathology which the helpee finds particularly painful and has, therefore, denied. If the early helping interviews can be seen as those during which the helpee is encouraged to present himself, *as he sees himself,* and if they also comprise a negotiation period during which the helpee needs to perceive that the helper is a helpful nurturant human being who can be trusted, then the preponderance of **Weakness** confrontations offered by the low facilitators is clearly inappropriate and often inaccurate. This becomes even more clear when it is realized that *the low-level helpers used Weakness confrontations with their hospitalized patients more than they used any other type of confrontations.* Thus, the lows used a preponderance of **Weakness** confrontations with those helpees least amenable to helping and least able to tolerate such confrontations. In addition, such confrontations were offered by helpers rated as extremely cold and ingenuine. Finally, such confrontations were offered by helpers rated as unempathic, which again calls into question not only the appropriateness but also the *accuracy* of such a focus on patient pathology.*Given the context of lower than minimally responsive conditions, and few compensatory Strength confrontations, we are convinced that the use of Weakness confrontations by the low level-helpers is a specific in-therapy behavior which leads to helpee deterioration.*

Action Confrontations

Like **Strength** confrontations, the number of **Action** confrontations was fairly small. Across the two helper

81

groups, students received significantly more **Action** confrontations than patients. As we mentioned earlier, this seems clinically appropriate since students, being healthier and not institutionalized, have more opportunities to interact with significant others, and under such circumstances, **Action** confrontations as early as the first interview seem relevant to their lives. We were surprised at the fairly modest correlations between **Strength** and **Action** confrontations. We had expected that one function of a **Strength** confrontation, perhaps quite early in the first hour, for example, would be to prepare the helpee for a subsequent **Action** confrontation. In any event, there seems to be only a modest relationship between a helper's use of these two confrontation categories. Our listening to the tape recordings led us to believe that, like **Strength** confrontations, greater use of **Action** confrontations would have been appropriate. However, in keeping with our earlier caution that precipitous helper or helpee action may be worse than no action at all, particularly early in helping, it seems that the helper in our sample erred on the more responsible side, if error is a fair judgment. *Nevertheless, we believe that Action Confrontations, in the context of below minimally responsive conditions, a clear lack of Strength confrontations, and a large number of Weakness confrontations, also is a specific helper behavior which leads to client deterioration.* In such a context, the low-functioning helper's encouragement of action would lead not only to precipitous but often inaccurate interaction with his helpee's significant others. The result could be a clear reaffirmation of *the* central neurotic distortion that the client and his significant others are unable to interact and change, in other words, that they are impotent and must remain so.

Over time in effective helping, we would expect an increase in the use of **Strength** and **Action** confrontations, and we would expect the increase to be related positively to helpee outcome if offered in a highly responsive context. We would also expect that both confrontations would be relatively more effective with out-patients rather than in-patients. Recent work on "assertion therapy" *(e.g., Lazarus, 1968, 1969; and, Lomont, Gilner, Spector and Skinner, 1969)* bears on this point. Working with hospitalized patients who were not schizophrenic, Lomont, et al *(1969)* for instance, found that group therapy which focused on role-played assertive behavior, as opposed to traditional insight-oriented group therapy, produced somewhat greater improvement over a six-week period. Since the number of patients in each group was small *(7 in the insight, and 5 in the assertive groups, respectively)* and the differences were moderate, the findings should be seen as suggestive. Nevertheless, the data support our general expectations regarding **Strength** and **Action** confrontations since "assertion therapy" techniques appear to include similar characteristics. Again, people do what they are trained to do. Generally, we see **Strength** and **Action** confrontations providing an ego-enhancing experience for helpees in the hour. In addition, we see these confrontations as helper behaviors which, if used appropriately, can increase the helpee's effectiveness with his significant others outside the therapy hour. That the effectiveness of these confrontations may be relatively greater for out- rather than in-patients follows from our earlier opinion that out-patients have greater opportunities to interact with significant others *and* from our suspicion that such confrontations would lead to patient behavior in a hospital setting which might be "healthier" in an objective sense but which might be viewed as maladaptive by a typical hospital staff.

An exciting consideration is that the use of **Strength** and **Action** confrontations may demand greater sensitivity to the helpee's "phenomenological world" than use of the other confrontation categories since they very well may lead more directly to changes in helpee behavior outside the helping hour. *Thus, the confronting helper must be acutely aware of how life is* *lived, and must be willing to be responsible for his actions.* In other words, he must be more of a social planner and manipulator than has been emphasized previously. Schematically, helping attempts to increase a helpee's assertive behavior with his signficant others includes two stages: **1.** encouragement of a general increase in such helpee behavior both in and outside of the hour and a detailed examination of these behaviors when they occur; and, **2.** after a general increase has been effected and the helpee has become more assertive in perhaps a somewhat indiscriminate manner, the helper must help the helpee to monitor these behaviors so that they are appropriate to the situation. The helpee must learn to discriminate among significant others with whom these behaviors will be successful. The helpee must be trained to initiate as he must be trained to respond. Careful monitoring is required because the helpee, after initially resisting his assertive or aggressive self, usually becomes assertive and aggressive in a number of situations where such behavior might not be in his best interests. The helper must be "alive" enough himself to discern that a tyrannical supervisor, for example, is never going to be able to allow his helpee to be assertive. More frequently, the helpee needs to be trained to respond before he initiates. The helper must also be willing to intervene and teach his helpee to discriminate among his significant others — those who are willing to let him be more assertive and those who must be "manipulated" or simply ignored. This two-stage model of the development of assertive behavior, which involves both a general increase and a subsequent responsible modification and discrimination of assertive behavior, forces the helper to be more directly his helpee's agent and more knowledgeable about, and sensitive to, his helpee's life outside the helping hour. Inevitably, and this is our major point, use of **Strength** and **Action** confrontations involves the helper's clear understanding of his and his helpee's life style and commitment to a helping process which extends far beyond the confines of his office, school or home. The helper in a hospital setting, for example, may also have to confront his colleagues on his patient's behalf. This position is in sharp contrast to attitudes held by a number of therapists. Goldman and Mendele *(1969)* asked a national sample of practicing psychotherapists to describe themselves, a preferred client, a cured client, and a normal person, on Gough's Adjective Check List. Among other findings, two-thirds of the self-concepts attributed by the therapists to themselves and their preferred clients differentiated between therapists and preferred clients significantly. *More than* two-thirds of the self-concepts differentiated between the therapists and their cured clients. Goldman and Mendele concluded that the therapists in their sample did not see either preferred or cured clients as resembling themselves, and more to the point, that these therapists clearly did not use themselves as reference points in setting therapy goals. Anything less must be suspect. At the least, most therapists have grave doubts about who they are and cannot use themselves as helping tools.

Sequence of Types of Confrontation

A potent action-oriented helping experience, based on deep levels of understanding, teaches the helpee to act more helpfully towards others in his life.

Having changed his behavior, the helpee can now not only change others to perceive him differently, but he can change them also. By having been acted upon and by learning to act upon himself, he can now trust himself to act upon others.

The former helpee has learned how to act on another person and increase the probability that the action will not only be helpful, but that the person acted upon will, in turn, learn to act constructively for himself and others. Both learn to do so because the first confrontations by a high-functioning helper are extensions of deep levels of understanding of the helpee filtered through the experience of a person who lives more effectively than the helpee. That is, all confrontations are increasingly responsive. The helpee wants most of all to be able to act and to live more fully.

Carkhuff *(1969)* points out that, over all, the sequence of helping moves from exploration, to understanding, to action. In the same manner, so does the sequence of confrontations.

Based on Carkhuff's model for helping *(1969)*, the confrontation model would be a segment of Carkhuff's third phase of helping, the action phase. The confrontation sequence, along with other initiative and action oriented dimension would be:

Carkhuff's Phase III: The Sequence of Confrontations

Although Experiential confrontations are employed by the high-level functioning helper throughout helping, they appear to be the type employed first. They appear again whenever the process of helping is recycled, that is, after a confrontation which elicits new material that requires exploration and deeper understanding.

In general, helper initiated **Experiential** and **Didactic Confrontations** elicit helpee self-exploration in terms of how the helpee experiences himself, in terms of how the helper experiences him, and how the helpee experiences himself in light of more accurate information about himself, others or areas of work, etc. When helpee exploration is self-sustaining, *as in Carkhuff's model,* he is ready to be confronted with his strengths and weaknesses. These confrontations elicit helpee understanding. Within the context of the helper's experience of him, new information, and the material uncovered as a result of his own exploration, the **Strength** and **Weakness** confrontations facilitate helpee understanding of himself at new levels. When the helpee volunteers new understandings of himself, he signals the helper that he is ready to act on his understanding, *as in Carkhuff's model.* Only then are **Action** confrontations likely to be effective.

In summary, our confrontation "model" includes two aspects. The most effective sequence of confrontations moves from an emphasis on **Experiential** and **Didactic** confrontations toward an emphasis on **Weakness** and **Strength** confrontations during the middle period within Carkhuff's third phase of helping where **Action** confrontations predominate.

From another view, we are also suggesting that a predominance of **Experiential** and **Didactic** confrontations would constitute "office-limited psycho therapy" and decrease the probability that new helpee learned behaviors would be generalized to other "real" life situations. The addition of **Strength** and **Action** confrontations expand the experience and may be viewed as "life-expanding psycho therapy".

The preconditions to effective helper confrontations revolve around depth of helper understanding of his helpee and his ability to communicate his understanding. Following confrontation, the effective helper delivers appropriate follow-through which may involve any combination of: interchangeable reflections, high levels of empathic responses, and/or directionful action-oriented confrontations.

6

Confrontation in Helping and Life

*"What applies in an honest helping effort applies in
life. What applies in life among growing and honest
people applies in helping!"*

Beyond what we have learned from the research
material presented in the earlier chapters, we have
learned as much or more from our listening to tapes of
hundreds of helper-helpee, teacher-student, parent-child,
and husband-wife interactions. In the remainder of this
chapter, we attempt to spell out our experiential
learnings as they were influenced by our research.

The basic core of this book rests on the belief that
unless the parties to any significant human relationship
press themselves and each other to deeper levels of
honesty and moment-to-moment contact, the relationship and the individuals will not grow. Further, the
likely path will be one of deterioration within a context
of mutual self-destruction.

At the highest levels, a growing person and a growing
relationship is highly conditional. Full honesty requires
persons who are fully committed to personal growth at
any cost. Full honesty, independent of anticipated
responses, *except with the most fragile,* valid or invalid,
sets the stage for greater self-definition, perhaps the
most vivid aspect of growth. The resulting momentary
closeness or distance emerges as an experience of
knowing one's self at the deepest levels — alone and
with others, free of the "should's" and "should not's",
social-cultural myths or injury and insult to one's basic
commitment to grow.

There is a second assumption which aided us in the
formulations of our research and generalizations. A
person is often less than who he can be because others
in his life could not or did not validate his experience;
neither could they act on themselves or others constructively. A large number of people grow up starved for
even minimal levels of understanding, genuineness,
respect and love *(Carkhuff, 1969).* Others who become
victimized are the products of much more subtle ways
and means of denial and starvation. They are exposed to

88

parents, teachers, counselors, helpers and employers who are, themselves, victims. These "helper-victims" excuse their inability to act constructively by postulating that each of us protects a core within that should not be shared or touched. Clinical experience teaches us that this inner, untouchable core is invariably something the person experiences as ugly, evil, and, hence, destructive. A few persons experience it as all that they have of what was once beautiful to them. This protection of, or "respect" for, the other person's inner core arises out of a pseudo-respect rather than the basic ingredients with which persons flourish. It is an appeal for a contract: I will not expose who you really are if you will not expose who I am *(Carkhuff and Berenson, 1967)* and/or if I expose or touch you, I know I will act to destroy.

There is, however, another side of this. The healthier among us keep something of ourselves from others because we sense that they will use and abuse rather than respect and love. The lesson is simple: We have learned that there are too few whom we can trust with who we really are at the deepest levels. For the most part, this may be adaptive in a cruel and neurotic world. It enables a person to experience deterioration at a rate slower than his more vulnerable brothers. With no interpersonal outlet for who we really are, even the more healthy enter into the "mutual non-exposure" pact in one way or another *(Carkhuff, 1969)*. The deterioration for even the stronger partly comes from the fact that any such agreement does not allow for personal emergence or growth.

How, then, do we discriminate between those who confront to deny us our human substance and emergence, allowing us at best only to survive, and those who, in confronting us share our experience and life by nurturing what is strong and attacking what is ugly and weak? What are the qualifications?

Those Who Are Entitled to Confront: Qualifications

1. *Only those who demonstrate deep levels of*

understanding which go far beyond what is
being said are potential sources of nourishment
and may be entitled to confront.

There is extensive evidence that confrontation based
upon deep levels of understanding results in a more full
and immediate exchange between the parties involved.
Confrontation without such understanding is not only
more likely to be inaccurate in content and affect, but
also destructive *(Carkhuff, 1969; Carkhuff and Berenson,
1967).* Only the deepest understanding will allow the
helper to discriminate between what is destructive in the
life and phenomenology of the helpee and what is
constructive. The foundation of trust does not come
from confrontation but from knowing the other person
truly understands and can communicate his understanding and is willing to act when the second party can not
act. Confrontation based on understanding serves as the
basis for respect. It is also the basis for establishing the
helper as a potent reinforcer *(Carkhuff, 1967).*

2. *Only those who demonstrate deep and
appropriate changing levels of regard and affect
are potential sources of nourishment and may
be entitled to confront.*

Those who offer a steady unchanging level of regard
and/or affect communicate to the helpee that he, the
helpee, cannot have an impact on the helper *(Carkhuff
and Berenson, 1967).* The helper in this instance serves as
a model for not acting upon the world: a condition that
can only lead to experiencing the self as increasingly
more impotent and, hence, cruel and destructive. Unchanging levels of regard and affect also suggest that the
basis for the relationship is techniqued. The helpee
consciously or unconsciously knows that his helper is a
psychopath at best. At worst he fears the implication of
his own feelings or is not in tune with them at all. The
helpee comes to know that the helper is himself a
helpee. *Any ensuing interaction is a series of denying
exchanges between two victims.*

Helper affect must be at first suspended and then

90

shared as the helper gains in understanding of the helpee, and it must be real. Helper respect moves from unconditional regard to conditional regard as his understanding of the helpee grows *(Carkhuff, 1969)*. Here, the helper communicates that he never acts independent of the helpee, that he acts and judges appropriately with growing direction, involvement, and demands upon himself and the helpee. Increasingly, and in a graduated way, the helper respects that which commands respect. Increasingly, and in a graduated way, he is intolerant of anything in the helpee and the relationship which does not demand that the parties involved be the best they can be, helper and helpee. At the most intimate moments of highest regard, the helper is a full participant with joy and pain rather than an exploitive manipulator. The essential message to the helpee is that the helper regards himself conditionally and offers no less to those he is committed to serving, even at the risk of losing the helpee.

   3.   *Only those who are physically robust and live fully from a high level of energy are potential sources of nourishment and may be entitled to confront.*

To confront and deal with the impact of constructive confrontation necessitates immense energy, durability and size. Because confrontation based on understanding is a full and real experience, it must be met and dealt with fully. Fatigue and loss of persistence during what may be a lengthy encounter results in an abandonment, all too common, in the life of a helpee. The initiation of a confrontation offers promise; its premature conclusion is another in a long series of broken promises. The helper then becomes just another who has nurtured false hopes in the helpee.

By failing to deliver and follow through, the helper serves as a model who depicts the world as a place requiring only apparency of delivery. He creates the impression that real delivery, by its omission, is unwanted and dangerous.

The helpee initially and periodically raises two basic questions: **a.** Does the helper have anything I want? and; **b.** Given my circumstances, could the helper make it better than I? *(Carkhuff and Berenson, 1967; and, Carkhuff, 1971).*

If the helper presents an image of fatigue and physical weakness, the helpee knows the whole process is a lie. In other words, the helper in many ways is asking or telling the helpee that over a time, the helpee will look and live like the helper. At one level or another, the helpee decides if he wishes to look and live like the helper. If the helpee chooses to stay with a sick looking helper, the helpee chooses to die. We become physically what we are psychologically. To a large extent, the most effective therapies include a physical conditioning program *(Carkhuff, 1971).*

4. Only those who love what they respect and respect those whom they love are potential sources of nourishment and may be entitled to confront.

Those who have become a party to the "mutual non-exposure" contract have agreed to ask others to be less than what they can be and, in turn, have agreed to be less than what they can be. In time, this conscious choice generates not only contempt for others but contempt for one's self. Thus, we observe the basic source of the neurotic's cruelty toward others and himself. Anyone who accepts the neurotic's terms, to be less than who he can be, is loved for not growing and held in disrespect for entering the agreement in the first place. The neurotic knows that only a person reaching for his full potential would never become a party to the "mutual non-exposure" contract. Those outside the agreement are never loved by the neurotic, but they are respected.

The helper, in the early phases of helping, has a choice: Be less than who he can be and win the love of the neurotic. Those who feel they can win the love and respect of the neurotic are themselves victims. Victims

92

can only help others to become victims.

Love without respect is license to abuse. When the license is revoked, the neurotic is furious. He withdraws his love, and in time his respect, if the other party is resolute in not allowing anyone, even himself, the right to violate his constructive growth.

Only those who are themselves growing can experience genuine joy in another's emergence and growth. The growing person may at appropriate moments demand deeper and deeper levels of honesty in the form of confrontation from those significant to him. Such a confrontation comes from an intimate knowledge of who he is, and who he is confronting.

The person who has ceased to grow, himself, knows he is deteriorating. The only thing he asks of others is that they deteriorate with him. He must then move to undermine, neutralize, slander, and destroy any growing person or any aspect of a person that is growing. His successful deleterious efforts produce the twisted rewards of non-exposure; his failure to undermine or destroy the growing is his only ray of hope.

Only those committed to their own constructive and creative personal emergence have the potential to confront constructively. Only those who act on themselves constructively are able to act constructively on others in the form of confrontation or in any other way.

Those Who Are Not Entitled to Confront

1. Those committed to survival can only act destructively and are not sources of nourishment and are not entitled to confront.

Although they experience the full implications of living as a highly conditional existence, those committed only to survival do not understand or entertain the possibility of personal emergence. They have not enjoyed earlier periods characterized by understanding and unconditional regard from significant others.

For the underprivileged, the struggle for survival is familiar. The mysteries of growth are unfamiliar because

93

the conditions for growth have been withheld. Promises of growth are held in distrust because promises in the past have not been fulfilled. Confrontation in this context involves little consideration for the consequences of what follows confrontation simply because there really is not anything to lose. For those who have enjoyed some measure of the conditions and opportunities necessary for growth, and for those who have experienced fulfilled promises, embracing a survival state constitutes another strategy to avoid the exposure of their dulled affect, distorted motives, and lack of competencies. Their lack of self-regard convinces them that they are entitled to no more than survival.

When a person takes more or less than what he is entitled to, he is self-destructive and adds more refuse to that which he wishes not to see or have others see in him. Growth in others only forces him to anticipate that those hidden aspects of his nature and history may become public. Rather than allowing this to happen, he chooses neuroticism, undermining the growth of others, fear, cruelty and even his own death. Those committed solely to survival, experience anything of real potency as a threat to survival. Movement in life can, for them, only have the apparency of growth. Confrontation must also be an apparency of confrontation. It must be short-lived, weak, and self-neutralizing — leaving no tangible benefits or change.

The growing and whole person *(Carkhuff and Berenson, 1967)* values another person's potential for growth more than the other person does. The final test of the helpee is likely to be an effort to turn this against the helper by withholding constructive behavior in order to place the helper on the helpee's schedule. This moment provides the effective helper an opportunity to risk the relationship and demonstrate in no uncertain terms that he will not and cannot become the helpee's victim, if the helping process is placed on the helpee's terms and not the helpers. This is not to say that the helper ceases to respond to the helpee's needs. The helper spends the

94

initial phases of helping doing mainly that — responding *(Carkhuff, 1969).* At still a deeper level, when the helper refuses to allow the helpee to turn his (the helper's) virtues against him, he, the helper, is exhibiting profoundly deep levels of empathic understanding of the helpee. It is the helpee's failure to "take" the helper that provides the helpee with a real choice and a possibility to grow. It tells the helpee that there is, after all, a source of strength in the world that will not be employed to violate him.

> *2. Those who have lost contact with their own experience can only react and are not sources of nourishment and are not entitled to confront.*

Confrontation, unlike the responsive dimensions such as empathy, emerges from the helper's experience of the helpee rather than the helpee's experience of himself. Confrontation gives the helping process concrete directionality by providing the helpee with a potent reinforcer who can and will act on another to achieve constructive ends. Beyond this, the helpee now knows that if he is to achieve more effective levels of living, he, too, must learn to act on his world and his experience of that world.

The helper who offers confrontation without being in full contact with his experience of himself and the helpee can only employ confrontation as an impersonal technique. The resulting interaction is likely to be irrelevant and, therefore, destructive. Most typically, the confrontation by such a helper appears to focus on the real or fabricated pathology of the helpee. In reality, it is often a reflection of the pathology of the helper.

If the helper has no experience of his own to draw upon, he has nothing through which to filter the feeling, content, and experience of the helpee's life. At that moment, the helper, as well as the helpee, is exposed. If there is no delivery, both parties know it. At best it is another unfulfilled promise for the helpee, at worst a fixing of an inappropriate and maladaptive response: he agrees to agree.

At a deeper level, the helper without the sensitivities necessary for constructive confrontation hesitates to act in the first place. His confrontations of helpee weaknesses or pathology provide him with material which appears to be beyond the helper's control and/or influence and beyond the influence of any real intervention or action of a personal nature. The low-level functioning helper is himself a victim and can only relate to and reinforce the helpee for being a victim. The victim knows that all acting on the world is destructive, for in the past whenever he has acted, it has been destructive.

The entire experience, attempted confrontation by a low-level helper, brings both parties into deeper contact with their helplessness and impotence: the very reasons for seeking help in the first place. In this and many other ways, the helping experience is no different than the experience of their daily lives: constant and vivid reminders that they cannot function to service themselves or others constructively. Hence, they both develop behaviors that provide only the apparency of acting as well as philosophies that appear to justify not acting. The essence of what they are doing and saying is: "If I act, I know it will be destructive. If I only appear to act, I am only observing the pain I and others experience." They settle for the latter, of course: to be observers of human experience, non-intervening distorting observers, knowing full well that in their apparent action or non-action, they act to destroy. Characteristically, they will do anything to avoid being held responsible for not acting even at the sacrifice of their helpee, a constructive actor, or themselves.

Perhaps, at still a deeper level, not being in contact with their experience is a sham. The fact is they are aware that if they translate into action how they experience their world and themselves, they must destroy.

For these persons all action is destructive.

3. Those who hold allegiances which are stronger than their commitment to construc-tive and creative personal emergence are not potential sources of nourishment and are not entitled to confront.

Behavior justified on the grounds that it serves an allegiance stronger than the commitment to creative growth and constructive personal emergence is too often the accepted basis for giving vent to injustice. It is merely another ploy of those not growing to act out their distortions with impunity. The less than healthy person all too often attempts to put the focus on what is right or wrong for society or an institution in order to divert attention from who he is. The healthy person does not fear close scrutiny. The healthy person, how-ever, fully understands that few have the right to exam-ine or judge him, and that the great majority will distort what they see.

The emphasis for the helper is framed in the demand that those around him will not be accepted for less than what they can be. The helper's commitment beyond himself is toward persons, not de-personalized institu-tions.

In order to make this demand, the helper must understand the less healthy person more completely than the less healthy person understands himself. This is possible because his self-understanding is free of distortions; hence, there is no contamination of his understanding of others.

Without this level of understanding and the ability to communicate it, confrontations initiated by the low-functioning helper and considered by the helpee confirm the low-functioning helper's conviction that the world asks only for cheap games and that after all, there are no healthy persons.

It is a demand of the healthier person that the less healthy person will not be accepted for less than he can be. The demand, if it is to be useful, must occur within the context of deep and full understanding. That is, the healthier person does have the potential for understanding the less healthy person more completely than the less healthy person knows himself. Without this depth of understanding and the ability to communicate it, confrontations in the form of demands are at best a hit-and-miss proposition. At worst, it is an experience confirming that there are no healthy persons in this world.

Confrontation, without a base of deep understanding of the helpee, sets the stage for the helpee to employ a wide variety of survival techniques. With only a knowledge of the techniques for survival and the lack of ability to tune in to other's experiences, the low-functioning helper, when he confronts, aids the helpee to employ a variety of diversionary tactics: 1. to avoid what he needs most: seeking a relationship with a high-functioning helper after leaving the low-functioning helper; 2. to destroy what he needs most: he will be more likely to distort the experience of meeting a real helper after his experience with the low-functioning helper; 3. to demand inexhaustible responsiveness from others while abusing most those who respond; 4. to pose as a victim of a high-functioning helper is his last line of defense.

These are some of the characteristics of the neurotic's style of life that brought him to helping in the first place. If like the great majority of helpees, he encounters a low-functioning helper, these characteristics are confirmed and solidified. If he encounters a high-functioning helper, these characteristics are understood and confronted. The helpee's secrets are now public. His helper has provided him with an alternate style of life, and, perhaps for the first time, the helpee has a choice.

Growing Skills

In essence then, only those who are committed to their own growth can experience genuine joy in another's emergence and growth and be a potential source of nourishment. The helper wants the helpee to live as he does: if the helper is growing, he will do all he can to promote growth. If the helper is deteriorating, he will do all he can to promote deterioration. Each kind of helper is fully aware of who he is and what he delivers to the patient.

There are other criteria which we have presented throughout. Here, however, we wish to explore the broader implication and meanings of this struggle to understand. Only the fully honest relationship can engender a full separateness in its closeness. That is, to leave the child, patient, spouse or friend untouched communicates simply that there are parts of him and ourselves we cannot or do not wish to know more fully or to make public. But only by knowing fully and sharing our experience of the helpee can we validate his experience and existence. This confirmation of experience and existence constitutes the beginnings of self-definition, direction, and independent identity.

Only a person whose experience has been validated by a healthy person or persons early in life or at some crisis point can move on to meet the next crisis with greater courage and creative action. He has acquired the repertoire of responses — *skills* — to do so. The others, like low-functioning helpers, have only a limited response available and are therefore less likely to cope with crises.

Facilitative confrontation is a set of skills. Like other skills, they must be learned. The honest and full confrontation initiated by a potent reinforcer (one who really understands) constitutes the conditions by which helpees learn these skills via modeling. *Self-definition and direction are directly related to the kind, quality and quantity of skills available in the time of crises.*

Personal emergence starts when the child learns that

he can contribute — *act* — physically, emotionally, and intellectually. These three sets of skills constitute the repertoire of responses he attempts to integrate in new ways to meet crises. The greater the number of skills in each area, the greater the probability for successful resolution of the crises. The high-functioning helper provides the helpee with a model of a person who can make such integrated physical, emotional, and intellectual responses, drawn from an ever-growing number of skills. His confrontations are new, unique to himself and the helpee.

The low-functioning helper with his limited number of poor quality responses employs confrontation as an irresponsible venting of infantile impulses, stereotyped and unchanging from person to person.

Confrontation initiated by a healthy helper is a skill based on a large and growing repertoire of responses, integrated creatively. These responses are gleaned from his experience of the helpee, himself; training; and his own willingness to risk in order to grow and learn. Confrontation emerging from this broad base serves to set the stage for a fully immediate, intense, uniquely personal interaction. Within this context, the full experiential confrontation provides no protection from social-professional roles and games. The participants are exposed in all their strengths and weaknesses: in all their constructive and destructive impulses.

Confrontation and the World We Live In

Confrontation in life as well as helping has become a verbal exchange designed to win a verbal game with the use of debate techniques. Rarely does it constitute an honest act. Even less frequently does confrontation constitute an effort to promote action for both parties. In more intense situations, confrontation is employed to expose and defeat so that the confronter experiences triumph and the person confronted, humiliation. For the most part, the constructive uses of confrontation are foreign. Only when confrontation is employed as a defensive measure is it completely acceptable, or when a group leader once gives permission to confront without regard to meaning, understanding or outcome. This is most vivid in those forms of encounter or sensitivity groups where the leader encourages the venting of venom by middle-aged adolescents who appear much like young vultures experiencing their first taste of blood.

In more conventional forms of helping, helpers are allowed or encouraged to confront in only a few situations. For example, they have license to confront character disorders in short-term crises situations, acting out delinquents, and aggressive face of patients. Even in these situations, the confrontation is rarely honest or full. When it is employed, it comes off more like a game or gimmick. One must give pause to wonder who is the real psychopath.

When employed consistently and used independently of high levels of empathic understanding, confrontation is negative and hostile. Within this context, the confronter may very well be a psychopath. Some even accept a fee for confronting like this and encourage others to do so.

Some Broader Issues of Personal and Social Responsibility

Most experiences emanating from helping which initially began as an honest human experience are later transformed into a manipulative technique and a game. The employment of confrontation as a gimmick is amply illustrated in the writings and reports of T-, Sensitivity and Encounter groups *(Carkhuff, 1971)*. Again, confrontation, in and out of helping when it does occur, is frequently implemented as a game independent of high levels of empathic understanding. That's what makes the use of these procedures a game in the hands of the average helper and they know it; they know they do not understand the helpee.

The most frequent tool of the low-functioning helper constitutes a set, *rather small,* of questions. When he occasionally employs another technique, he presents that technique as his orientation.

The average helper cannot afford a full and open confrontation with his helpee because he cannot afford exposing the fact that he knows he has been cheating his patient. Thus, his confrontations occur rather infrequently and when they occur, they are not even related to the series of questions he has been asking. The confrontation has been, like the questions, formulated long before he ever heard of or saw the helpee. For most of these low-functioning helpers *(those that employ confrontation at all),* the incongruity between his questions and the confrontation are designed to make a desperate helpee think that his helper has something in mind that the helpee has not become aware of. From the low-functioning helper's point of view, the confrontation following his stereotyped questions is done with the hope of eliciting abnormal behavior, *and it most certainly does,* and of intimidating the patient so that he will not dare to confront his helper.

The average helper is convinced that if he confronts *(or was confronted)* fully, he would have to do so as a person. Without his armament of stupid questions, he, like the patient, will act destructively. What he settles for is a destructive approach he thinks will absolve him of his responsibility for destroying. He "sounds" professional. That is, without his role of expert and stripped of his status, when standing alone, he is, and he knows he is, a destructive person. In the hands of such helpers, roles and status are tools which assist him in his effort to avoid personal responsibility. From his vantage point, there is no consideration of the possibility that there are those who can risk full exposure in a full experiential confrontation. In addition, he does not entertain the possibility that such an encounter can be employed as a constructive experience for both the helpee and the helper. It is not possible for the low-functioning helper to entertain the possibility that another human lives honestly and lives more effectively than his helpee. The low-functioning helper is, and experiences himself as, a helpee — *patient, victim.*

Only when the helper knows he lives more honestly and effectively than his helpee can he, the helper, confront his helpee at the deepest and fullest level and deal fully with the necessary follow-through. That is, the aftermath of an experiential confrontation most frequently uncovers new material, and, hence, there is a necessity for the helper to return to responding before reaching for new directions and more intense levels of immediacy.

A Few Additional Points

1. The less than effective person is essentially an observer and a poor one at that. He views confrontation as acting on impulse to defeat others. His impulses are largely dictated by fear and as a consequence lead to destructive action. He assumes this to be true for everyone else. The role of the observer-judge who never commits a direction of his own is adopted. The implication is that the observer-judge is superior to the doer. Thus, the ineffective helper is convinced that in order to avoid being destructive, he must avoid acting, and he is correct in his case. His actions, based on little or no understanding, distorted perceptions, and the awareness that he cannot help anyone, even himself, are most likely to be deleterious. Yet his inability to act constructively is by itself destructive, and he knows this too. So when he can, he will act to neutralize the efforts of effective helpers.

2. The effective person is an actor, a doer, and understands and welcomes the responsibility for his action. Because the majority of people are observer-judges, the effective person is ready to deal and live with the fact that he may be compelled to live on the periphery of society *(Carkhuff and Berenson, 1967)*. Unlike the observer-judge, he knows he must often pay a price for his growth and learning. He knows he often learns the most from acting on what he fears the most and learns the most from acting on what he loves the most *(Carkhuff and Berenson, 1967)*.

3. The effective person experiences no fear of exposure nor is he motivated to seek exposure. He can and must live in contact with his own expanding experience and come into contact with the experience of another person. He does not question his responsibility for confronting and his obligation to follow-through with even higher levels of helping conditions. He is keenly aware of the role model he provides his helpees but is not dominated or neutralized by this awareness. He is thus free to make each encounter a new experience for himself and his helpee.

4. The effective person is not dependent upon others or society to define his identity or function in life. His function and actions in life are defined in terms of how he experiences his world. He knows his perceptions are not distortions, and in a world largely governed by observer-judges, he has no alternative but to expand this experience and act on it in order to continue to grow. The effective person defines himself.

5. The effective person knows he cannot live and grow while seeking the approval and adulation from the large majority of observer-judges. He knows the majority are not fit to judge or know him. He knows that to seek approval would put him on other's schedules and hence render him as impotent and as destructive as they, who only withhold approval for creative action and give approval for pseudo-action. He often stands and lives alone, even at the risk of losing a relationship with a helpee.

6. The effective person while trusting his own motives, impulses and actions, leaves room to trust the motives, impulses and actions of other effective persons. Because he seeks to learn and not distort, his accumulated experience and his ability to make appropriate discriminations allow him the time to continually increase intimate encounters with those who are also growing. He understands that such encounters will demand the full employment of his resources and the resources of the other person. By confronting a growing person appropriately, he offers full human equality and creates the conditions for even more intense encounters.

7. At the moment of confrontation, the effective person communicates that he not only trusts himself but is open to trusting the helpee. He enables the helpee to experience his own potential for potency. The effective person may confront the helpee with what is constructive or confront to destroy what is keeping the helpee from growing. He does not confront merely to destroy the helpee or elicit pathological behavior. The effective person, while daring to confront, communicates that he does not fear what is destructive in the other person. The appropriate follow-through, higher levels of helping conditions, persistence in the confrontation, enables the helpee to not only experience his own potency, but to let go of his attempts to defeat the effective person's efforts to help. The less effective helper confronts to make the helpee experience impotency as he, the ineffective person, experiences it, and if he follows through, he does so to point this out in one way or another.

8. By taking action, the effective person encourages helpee action. There is the full realization that nothing often changes until both parties act on what they have come to understand. There is no learning without action *(Carkhuff and Berenson, 1967).* There is no understanding without action. There is no growth without action. There is no hope for intimacy without action. Both parties grow from the feedback resulting from their acts and both are better defined as persons.

9. After a full confrontation, both parties know that the helpee now has alternatives to his usual modes of responding. He has learned to translate understanding into action. He has learned a new skill. He has also learned that as hard as he has tried, he has not been able to injure or insult the helper's integrity and honesty. He has learned that after all, it is possible to intervene in another person's life creatively and constructively and that he now has the skill to intervene in his own life. He has learned that he cannot destroy his helper. Both the effective helper and the helpee have put all of their constructive and destructive forces on the line, and the constructive have outweighed the destructive.

10. *Helpee honesty, integrity and growth can only be encouraged by a responsible and whole person.* Perhaps for the first time the helpee has experienced crises and has emerged more confident, more directionful and more whole. He has come to know this because of the confidence and direction provided by his helper and the helper's ability to mobilize what was growing in both parties. Most important, such a relationship enables the helpee to accept responsibility for himself. The helpee knows he has been confronted and the confronter demanded change and that change occurred.

> Only those few who have the right to help,
> have the right to confront.
> Confrontation is never *necessary.*
> Confrontation is never *sufficient.*
> In the hands of those few who have the right
> to help, confrontation may be *efficient.*

references

Alexander, J. F., and Abeles, N. Dependency changes in psychotherapy as related to interpersonal relationships. **Journal of Consulting and Clinical Psychology**, 1968, **32**, 685-689.

Alger, I., and Hogan, P. Enduring effects of video tape playback experience on family and marital relationships. **American Journal of Orthopsychiatry**, 1969, **39**, 86-98.

Aspy, D. N., The study of three facilitative conditions and their relationships to the achievement of third grade students. Unpublished doctoral dissertation, University of Kentucky, 1965.

Bateson, G., Jackson, D. H., Jr., and Weakland, J. H. Toward a theory of schizophrenia. **Behavioral Science**, 1956, **1**, 251-264.

Begley, C. E., and Lieberman, L. R. Patient expectations of therapists' techniques. **Journal of Clinical Psychology**, 1970, **26**, 112-116.

Berenson, B. G., Carkhuff, R. R., and Myrus, P. An investigation of training effects on interpersonal functioning of undergraduate college students. **Journal of Counseling Psychology**, 1966, **13**, 441-446.

Berenson, B. G., Friel, T., and Mitchell, K. M. Factor analysis of therapeutic conditions for high- and low-functioning therapists. **Journal of Clinical Psychology**, 1970 *in press.*

Berenson, B. G., Mitchell, K. M., and Laney, R. Level of therapist functioning, types of confrontation, and type of patient. **Journal of Clinical Psychology**, 1968, **24**, 111-113.

Berenson, B. G., Mitchell, K. M., and Moravec, J. A. Level of therapist functioning, type of confrontation, and patient depth of self-exploration. **Journal of Counseling Psychology**, 1968, **15**, 136-139.

Boomer, D. C., and Goodrick, D. W. Speech disturbance and judged anxiety. **Journal of Consulting Psychology,** 1961, **25,** 160-164.

Bordin, E. S. Ambiguity as the therapeutic variable. **Journal of Consulting Psychology,** 1955, **19,** 9-15.

Boyd, H. S., and Sisney, V. Immediate self-image confrontation and change in self-concept. **Journal of Consulting Psychology,** 1967, **31,** 291-294.

Carkhuff, R. R. Facilitative genuineness in interpersonal processes: A scale for measurement. Unpublished research scale, University of Massachusetts, 1964a.

Carkhuff, R. R. Personally relevant concreteness or specificity of expression in interpersonal processes: A scale for measurement. Unpublished research scale, University of Massachusetts, 1964b.

Carkhuff, R. R., Self-exploration in interpersonal processes: A scale for measurement. Unpublished research scale, University of Massachusetts, 1964c.

Carkhuff, R. R., Toward a comprehensive model of counseling and psychotherapy. **Journal of Counseling Psychology,** 1967, **14,** 67-72.

Carkhuff, R. R., **Helping and Human Relations: A Primer for Lay and Professional Helpers. Vol. 1: Selection and Training and Vol. 2: Practice and Research.** New York: Holt, Rinehart and Winston, 1969.

Carkhuff, R. R., **The Development of Human Resources: Education, Psychology and Social Change.** New York: Holt, Rinehart and Winston, 1971.

Carkhuff, R. R., and Berenson, B. G., **Beyond Counseling and Psychotherapy.** New York: Holt, Rinehart, and Winston, 1967.

Cohen, J. Some statistical issues in psychological research. In Wolman, B. B. *Ed.* **Handbook of Clinical Psychology.** New York: McGraw Hill, 1965.

Cowen, E. L. Gardner, E. A., and Zax, M. **Emergent Approaches to Mental Health Problems.** New York: Appleton-Century-Crofts, 1967.

Danet, B. N. Self-confrontation in Psychotherapy Reviewed: Video tape playback as a clinical and research tool. **American Journal of Psychotherapy,** 1968, **22,** 245-257.

Danet, B. N. Impact of audio-visual feedback on group psychotherapy. **Journal of Consulting and Clinical Psychology,** 1969, **33,** 632.

Dibner, A. S. Cue-counting: A measure of anxiety in interviews. **Journal of Consulting Psychology,** 1956, **20,** 475-478.

Dole, A. A., Nottingham, J., and Wrightsman, L. S. Beliefs about human nature held by counseling, clinical and rehabilitation students. **Students of Counseling Psychology,** 1969, **16,** 197-202.

Duncan, D. B. Multiple range tests were correlated and heteroszedastic means. **Biometrics,** 1957, **13,** 164-176.

Ellis, A. **Reason and Emotion in Psychotherapy.** New York: Stuart, 1962.

Fairbairn, R. W. **An Object-relations Theory of Personality.** New York: Basic Books, 1954.

Frank, G. H. The effect of directive and non-directive statements by therapists on the content of patient verbalizations. **Journal of General Psychology,** 1964, **71,** 321-328.

Frank, J. **Persuasion and Healing.** Baltimore: Johns Hopkins University Press, 1961.

Freeman, R., and Grayson, H. M. Maternal attitudes in schizophrenia. **Journal of Abnormal and Social Psychology,** 1971, **27,** No. 2.

Friel, T. W. Factor analysis of levels of therapist functioning and confrontation. **Journal of Clinical Psychology,** 1971, **27,** No. 2.

Gardner, G. The psychotherapeutic relationship. **Psychological Bulletin,** 1964, **61,** 426-437.

Garner, H. H. A confrontation technique used in psychotherapy. **American Journal of Psychotherapy,** 1959, **8,** 18-34.

Garner, H. H. Interventions in psychotherapy in confrontation technique. **American Journal of Psychoanalysis,** 1962, **22,** 1-12.

Garner, H. H. Interventions in psychotherapy in confrontation technique. **American Journal of Psychotherapy,** 1966, **20,** 391-404.

Gladstein, G. A. Client expectations, counseling experience, and satisfaction. **Journal of Counseling Psychology,** 1969, **16,** 476-481.

Goldman, R. K., and Mendelsohn, G. A. Psychotherapeutic change and social adjustment; a report of a national survey of psychotherapists. **Journal of Abnormal Psychology,** 1969, **74,** 164-172.

Grant, D. A. Analysis-of-variance tests in the analysis and comparison of curves. **Psychological Bulletin,** 1956, **53,** 141-154.

Greenberg, R. P. Effects of pre-session information on perception of the therapist and receptivity to influence in a psychotherapy analogue. **Journal of Consulting and Clinical Psychology,** 1969, **33,** 425-429.

Greenberg, R. P., Goldstein, A. P., and Perry, M. A. The influence of referral information on patient perception in a psychotherapy analogue. **Journal of Nervous and Mental Disease,** 1970, **150,** 31-36.

Guntrip, H. **Personality Structure and Human Interaction.** London: Hogarth, 1961.

Hinkle, D. N. The change of personal constructs from the viewpoint of a theory of implication. Unpublished doctoral dissertation, Ohio State University, 1965.

Hobbs, N. Sources of gain in psychotherapy. **American Psychologist,** 1962, **17,** 18-34.

Hogan, P., and Alger, I. The impact of video tape recording on insight in group psychotherapy. **International Journal of Group Psychotherapy,** 1969, **19,** 158-164.

Howe, E. S. Anxiety-arousal and specificity: Rated correlates of the depth of interpretative statements. **Journal of Consulting Psychology,** 1962, **26,** 178-184.

Howe, E. S., and Pope, B. An empirical scale of therapist verbal activity level in the initial interview. **Journal of Consulting Psychology,** 1961, **25,** 510-520.

Isaacs, K. S., and Haggard, E. A. Some methods used in the study of affect — in psychotherapy. In Gottschalk, L. A. and Auerbach, A. H. *Eds.,* **Methods of Research in Psychotherapy.** New York: Appleton-Century-Crofts, 1966.

Kanzer, M., and Blum, H. P. Classical psychoanalysis since 1939. In Wolman, B. B. *Ed.,* **Psychoanalytic techniques: A handbook for the practicing psychoanalyst.** New York: Basic Books, 1967.

Karl, N. J., and Abeles, N. Psychotherapy process as a function of the time segment sample. **Journal of Consulting and Clinical Psychology,** 1969, **33,** 207-212.

Kaswan, J., and Love, L. R. Confrontation as a method of psychological intervention. **Journal of Nervous and Mental Disease,** 1969, **148,** 224-237.

Kell, B. L., and Mueller, W. J. **Impact and Change: A Study of Counseling Relationships.** New York: Appleton-Century-Crofts, 1966.

Kelly, G. A. **The Psychology of Personal Constructs, Vol. 1.** New York: Norton, 1955.

Kiesler, D. V. Some myths of psychotherapy research and the search for a paradigm. **Psychological Bulletin,** 1966, **65,** 110-136.

Krause, M. S., Fitzsimmons, M., and Wolfe, N. Focusing on the client's expectations of treatment: Brief report. **Psychological Reports,** 1969, **24,** 973-974.

Lazarus, A. A. Behavior rehearsal versus non-directive therapy versus advice in effecting behavior change. **Behavioral Research and Therapy,** 1966, **4,** 209-

Lazarus, A. A. Learning theory in the treatment of depression. **Behavioral Research and Therapy,** 1968, **6,** 83-89.

Lazarus, A. A. Variations in desensitization therapy. **Psychotherapy: Theory, Research and Practice,** 1968, **5,** 50-53.

Lennard, H., and Bernstein, A. **The Anatomy of Psychotherapy.** New York: Columbia University Press, 1960.

Lomont, J. F., Gilner, F. H., Spector, N. J., and Skinner, K. K. Group assertion training and group insight therapies. **Psychological Reports,** 1969, **25,** 463-370.

Mainord, W. A., Burk, H. W., and Collins, L. G. Confrontation versus diversion in group therapy with chronic schizophrenics as measured by a "positive incident" criterion. **Journal of Clinical Psychology,** 1965, **21,** 222-225.

Marcondes, D. New aspects of the clinical interview: Counter-transference difficulties. **Psychosomatic Medicine,** 1960, **22,** 211-217.

Mark, J. The attitudes of the mothers of male schizophrenic patients. **Journal of Abnormal and Social Psychology,** 1953, **42,** 185-189.

Matarazzo, J. D., Weitman, M., Saslow, G., and Weins, A. N. Interviewer influence on duration of interviewee speech. **Journal of Verbal Learning and Verbal Behavior,** 1963, **1,** 451-458.

McNair, D. M., and Lorr, M. An analysis of professed psychotherapeutic techniques. **Journal of Consulting Psychology,** 1964, **28,** 265-271.

Meyer, R. G. and Karon, B. P. A study of the schizophrenogenic mother concept by means of the TAT. **Psychiatry,** 1967, **30,** 163-179.

Mitchell, K. M. An analysis of the schizophrenogenic mother concept by means of the thermatic apperception test. **Journal of Abnormal Psychology,** 1968, **73,** 571-574.

Mitchell, K. M. Concept of pathogenesis in parents of schizophrenic and normal children. **Journal of Abnormal Psychology,** 1969, **74,** 423-424.

Mitchell, K. M. and Berenson, B. G. Differential use of confrontation by high and low-facilitative therapists. **Journal of Nervous and Mental Disease,** 1970, **151,** 303-309.

Mitchell, K. M. and Hall, L. A. Frequency and type of confrontation over time within the first therapy interview. **Journal of Consulting and Clinical Psychology,** 1971, **37,** 437-442.

Mitchell, K. M., Mitchell, R. M., and Berenson, B. G. Therapist focus on clients' significant others in psychotherapy. **Journal of Clinical Psychology,** 1970, **26,** 533-536.

Mitchell, Rosamond, M. Relationship between therapist response to therapist relevant client expressions and therapy process and client outcome. Unpublished doctoral dissertation, Michigan State University, East Lansing, Michigan, 1971.

Pallone, N. J., and Grande, P. P. Counselor verbal mode, problem relevant communication, and client rapport. **Journal of Counseling Psychology,** 1965, **12,** 359-365.

Paredes, A., Ludwig, K. D., Hassenfeld, I. N., and Cornelison, F. S. A clinical study of alcoholics using audio-visual self-image feedback. **Journal of Nervous and Mental Disease,** 1969, **148,** 449-456.

Pope, B., and Siegman, A. W. The effect of therapist verbal activity level and specificity on patient productivity and speech disturbance in the initial interview. **Journal of Consulting Psychology,** 1962, **26,** 489.

Rogers, C. R. **On Becoming a Person.** Boston: Houghton Mifflin, 1961.

Rogers, C. R., Gendlin, E. T., Kiesler, D. J., and Truax, C. B. **The Therapeutic Relationship and its Impact: A Study of Psychotherapy with Schizophrenics.** Madison, Wisconsin: The University of Wisconsin Press, 1967.

Rokeach, M. **Beliefs, Attitudes, and Values: A Theory of Organization and Change.** San Francisco: Jossey-Bass, 1968.

Russell, P. D., and Synder, W. U. Counselor anxiety in relation to amount of clinical experience and quality of affect demonstrated by clients. **Journal of Counseling Psychology,** 1963, **27,** 358-363.

Sandifer, M. G., Jr., Hordern, A., and Green, L. M. The psychiatric interview: The impact of the first three minutes. **American Journal of Psychiatry,** 1970, **126,** 968-972.

Siegman, A. W., and Pope, B. Effects of question specificity and anxiety-producing messages on verbal fluency in the initial interview. **Journal of Personality and Social Psychology,** 1965, **2,** 522-530.

Singer, E. **Key concepts in psychotherapy.** New York: Random House, 1965.

Sloane, R. B., Cristol, A. H., Peppernik, M. C., and Staples, F. R. Role preparation and expectation of improvement in psychotherapy. **Journal of Nervous and Mental Disease,** 1970, **150,** 18-26.

Stoller, F. H. Video tape feedback in the group setting. **Journal of Nervous and Mental Disease,** 1969, **148,** 457-466.

Strupp, H. H. **Psychotherapists in Action.** New York: Grune and Stratton, 1960.

Strupp, H. H. Nature of the psychotherapist's contribution to the treatment process. **Archives of General Psychiatry,** 1960, **3,** 219-231.

Sullivan, H. S. **Clinical Studies in Psychiatry.** New York: Norton, 1956.

Sundland, D. N., and Barker, E. N. The orientations of psychotherapists. **Journal of Consulting Psychology,** 1962, **26,** 201-221.

Thorne, F. C. **The Principles of Personality Counseling.** Brandon, Vermont: Journal of Clinical Psychology Press, 1950.

Thorne, F. C. Directive and eclectic personality counseling. In McCary, J. L. and Shier, D. **Six Approaches to Psychotherapy.** New York: Dryden, 1955.

Truax, C. B., and Mitchell, K. M. Research on certain therapist skills in relation to process and outcome. **In Handbook of Psychotherapy and Behavior Change.** Bergin, A. E., and Garfield, S. E. *Eds.,* New York: Wiley, 1971.

Truax, C. B., and Tatum, C. R. An extension from the effective psychotherapeutic model to constructive personality change in pre-school children. **Childhood Education,** 1966, **42,** 456-462.

Vesprani, G. J. Personality correlates to accurate empathy in a college companion program. **Journal of Consulting and Clinical Psychology,** 1969, **33,** 722-727.

Wagner, H. M., and Mitchell, K. M. Relationship between perceived instructors' accurate empathy, warmth, and genuineness and college achievement. **Discussion Paper,** Arkansas Rehabilitation Research and Training Center, University of Arkansas, 1969, **13.**

Wallach, M. S., and Strupp, H. H. Dimensions of psychotherapists' activity. **Journal of Consulting Psychology,** 1964, **28,** 120-125.

Whitaker, C. A., and Malone, T. B. **The Roots of Psychotherapy.** New York: McGraw-Hill, 1953.

Wiener, B. J. **Statistical Principles in Experimental Design.** New York: McGraw-Hill, 1962.

Other Works by Bernard G. Berenson

Berenson, B. G. and Carkhuff, R. R. **Sources of Gain in Counseling and Psychotherapy.** New York: Holt, Rinehart and Winston, 1967.

Carkhuff, R. R. and Berenson, B. G., **Beyond Counseling and Therapy.** New York: Holt, Rinehart, and Winston, 1967.

Berenson, B. G. **The Militant Humanism of Robert R. Carkhuff.** Amherst, Mass.: Human Resource Development Press, 1974.

Berenson, B. G. **Toward a Human Technology,** in press, Amherst, Mass.: Human Resource Development Press, 1974.

trainer series

teaching as treatment

an introduction to counseling & psychotherapy

robert r carkhuff, ph.d.
bernard g. berenson, ph.d.

carkhuff institute of human technology

9.95

Perhaps the most forceful and vital substantive contribution made to the helping field in this decade. This new HRD Press text by Drs. Carkhuff and Berenson provides the empirical bases, latest models and comprehensive system needed to go from model to outcome. Focusing on the learning processes, teaching skills, training programs and specific outcomes which define teaching as treatment, the authors explain and demonstrate how to establish concrete objectives in human resource development, monitor progress towards goals and assess ultimate outcomes. Also detailed is a comprehensive system which integrates both skill delivery and administrative support functions in a way that focuses directly on helpee outcomes.

Trainer's guide

the art of HELPING

an introduction to life skills

Robert R. Carkhuff, Ph.D.
&
Richard M. Pierce, Ph.D.

Based on 10,000 hours of training experience with over 50,000 people, this text brings you the potency and effective expertise needed to deliver helping skills. The text includes pre- and post-tests with rating scales for accurate diagnosis and evaluation. It explains why each skill is important and how it fits into the total helping process. It delivers action steps to guide the trainer in conducting training and think steps to give him or her the facility to deliver concrete feedback to correct trainee errors. Finally, the text explains how to integrate the HRD Training and Demonstration Videotapes into training to maximize the variety and depth of the training experience. 9.95

the art of DEVELOPING a CAREER

A Helper's Guide

Theodore W. Friel, Ph.D.
&
Robert R. Carkhuff, Ph.D.   9.95

For those of you who have accepted the challenge of teaching your helpees and students how to develop their own careers, this book lays out the materials you need to teach skills like:
How to expand career alternatives
How to develop and clarify personal values
How to choose the best career based on your values
How to see yourself through the job's "eyes"
How to prepare to meet and exceed the job's requirements
The Career Helper's Guide gives you the first steps you need to place your trainees on the jobs they want most.

Helpees need skills to make it in their worlds. The more varied your training programs, the more likely that your trainees will master those skills. These tapes deliver both models and skills using proven delivery methods to ensure mastery.

Dr. Carkhuff has created three basic training modules which you can use to introduce the skills model and training program to your own trainees and students.

Life Skills Model Videotapes

Helping Model Module: This videotape introduces the basic Carkhuff Model and deals in depth with the major sub-skills involved in Attending, Responding, Personalizing and Initiating. 1 hour, $250.00.

Problem Solving Model Module: This second videotape module reviews the Carkhuff Model and then expands this model to deal with and deliver to trainees the critical sub-skills entailed by decision-making. 1 hour, $250.00.

Program Development Model Module: Having reviewed the basic Carkhuff Model, the third videotape goes on to deal at length and in considerable detail with the specific sub-skills entailed by program development. 1 hour, $250.00.

Life Skills Videotape Set (above 3) $635.00

Dr. Carkhuff has prepared three interview tapes for advanced trainees which demonstrate the final and effective integration of helping skills. These tapes, like the other HRD Video tapes, allow the trainer to "stop the action" and explain important principles and behaviors for purposes of in-depth study and mastery.

Art of Helping Demonstration Videotapes

The Case of Jerry: In this hour-long interview with a young man who must make a critical decision in his own life, Dr. Carkhuff demonstrates the simultaneous use of all the specific advanced in-personal, decision-making and program development skills. This tape truly puts it all together! 1 hour, $250.00.

The Case of Jane: This taped interview with a young mother who is having child-rearing problems illustrates the use by Dr. Carkhuff of advanced responsive and initiative skills. ¾ hour, $200.00.

The Case of Manny: The subject of this hour-long tape is a young man experiencing a number of social and interpersonal difficulties. In helping him, Dr. Carkhuff demonstrates the use of advanced responsive and immediacy skills. 1 hour, $250.00.

Art of Helping Demonstration Set (above 3) $595.00

. Carkhuff serves a model trainer in these four videotape training modules, each of which discusses and illustrates the helping concepts in the depth needed by more advanced trainees. As with all of the HRD Videotapes, these half-hour modules will add to your understanding of the finer points of teaching specific helping skills.

Art of Helping Training Videotapes

Attending Skills Module: By discussing and demonstrating the specific skills of physical posturing, observing and listening, this videotape promotes trainees' ability to set the stage for effectiveness. $200.00.

Responding Skills Module: In this videotape, Dr. Carkhuff discusses and demonstrates the techniques involved in responding to content, feeling and meaning so that trainees can master these techniques for later use with their own helpees. $200.00.

Personalizing Skills Module: In this third videotape, Dr. Carkhuff explains and demonstrates the types of responses which will enable your trainees to personalize their helpees' unique behavioral deficits and move toward the clear definition of goals. $200.00.

Initiating Skills Module: In this final videotape, Dr. Carkhuff outlines the skills which trainees will need to use in operationalizing their helpees' goals and helping them to achieve these same goals. $200.00.

Art of Helping Training Videotape Set (above 4) $675.00

Dr. Carkhuff delivers an important selection and research tool, the HRD AUDIOTAPE PACKAGES, to today's helping professionals and concerned lay leaders. Designed to help you discriminate in detail the level and breadth of interpersonal expertise latent in client and helper populations you deal with.

Audio Cassette Tape Packages

These tapes have been developed in response to the ever-increasing demand for research scales and selection tests for interpersonal skills. These four sets of parallel pre- and post-tests involve a wide range of emotional categories and problem areas specifically drawn from the populations listed below. As a result, the tapes allow the trainer to diagnose those feelings and situations that are or are not handled effectively. In addition, they provide graduate students and faculty with detailed background information explaining how the scales and tapes can be used in research and training. Each tape is a half-hour long and comes complete with User's Guide and handsome case.

Teacher-Student Audio Tape Package:	$25.00
Counselor-Counselee Audio Tape Package:	$25.00
Correctional Helper-Inmate Audio Tape Package:	$25.00
Human Relations: Racism/Sexism Audio Tape Package:	$25.00
All Four Audiotape Packages:	$75.00

life skills series

This is a rational, self-explanatory text for individuals who want and need special expertise in Decision Making Skills. The book explains, demonstrates and allows you to practice the skills of Problem Definition, Goal Setting, Value Clarification and Alternative Selection and Evaluation. The **Art of Problem Solving** builds on the interpersonal skills in the **Art of Helping** to turn insights into choices of preferred courses of action.   5.95

the art of HELPING
an introduction to life skills

Robert R. Carkhuff

5.95

This is the number one best seller in counseling because it is straightforward, clearly written and well-illustrated for use by trainees in developing interpersonal skills. Designed to be easily integrated with the HRD Videotape Series for more in-depth training, **The Art of Helping** includes Attending Skills, Responding Skills, Personalizing Skills and Initiating Skills. The text has been successfully used by over 50,000 helpers in schools, colleges, mental health, industry and home settings.

5.95

This book teaches you how to go somewhere. How to achieve. How to reach your goals. It makes everything possible. It is meant for people, all people. Parents as well as children. Teachers as well as students. Counselors as well as clients. It is where everyone begins. Where they end depends upon the programs they develop.

Diagnostic skills, operationalized goal setting and skills concerning how t develop and implement step-by-ste programs give you **THE** winning strateg

how to help yourself

perspective series

Values are the beginning. Constructive institutional change comes only with systematic diagnosis and planning. Dr. Carkhuff's **Cry Twice!** is both a case study and a handbook of basic consulting skills. Topics considered relate directly to:

Staff selection and training
Development of treatment programs for clients
Implementation strategies

Cry Twice! demonstrates how to develop and implement large-scale institutional improvements by focusing on the most important facets of change—people, programs and their organization.

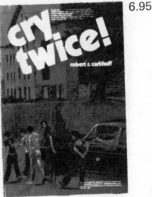

6.95

6.95

Human values are the living heart of any delivery system. Such values are crucial because they dictate the goals and the professional ethic involved in achieving these goals.

Belly to Belly, Back to Back is a collection of powerful essays, allegories and poetry by Bob Carkhuff. They present the world as he sees it—the **human** side of Human Technology, the values, principles, assumptions and philosophy of a militant humanist.

This book stimulates deep thought and self-exploration concerning the present state of the world, its implications for humankind's future and our responsibility for shaping that future.

Value judgements and effective action must culminate in a systematic research evaluation. Constructive and constant feedback is a necessary condition for personal growth and development.

"Confrontation is never necessary and never sufficient." But in the hands of those few helpers—and fewer trainers —who have the skills and, thus, the right to help and train, confrontation is **efficient.**

This book teaches you what you need to know about the uses and abuses of confrontation and demonstrates the use of empirical study to uncover the ingredients of effectiveness.

6.95

career skills series

the art of
DEVELOPING
a CAREER

A Student's Guide

Robert R. Carkhuff, Ph.D.
&
Theodore W. Friel, Ph.D.

3.45

3.95

6.95

These richly illustrated text-work-books are designed to teach your helpees the skills they need to expand career options, make their career choices and plan how to reach their career goal. They are sequenced for use with populations from grades 4-6 to junior high school and high school/college. They are the follow-up material which allows helpee-learners to review skills long after they've completed your course so that they can recycle and refine their career plans.

These books concretize career development into 100 behaviorally defined exercises and subskills to simplify your teaching and evaluation efforts. See the **Trainer Series** for a teacher-training version of these workbooks.

Students with these skills have been shown to stand a 90% better chance of getting hired than those who had not been trained.

GETAJOB

ROBERT R. CARKHUFF, Ph.D.
RICHARD M. PIERCE, Ph.D.
TED W. FRIEL, Ph.D.
DAVID G. WILLIS, M.A.

6.95

Helping your trainees and students to find themselves and to meet the requirements of their career choice is a first step. And helping them to land a job is the logical next step.

GETAJOB takes the mystery and failure out of teaching others to sell themselves and get jobs.

This is a clear workbook text designed to teach your students:

* How to use both work and school experiences to write a resume that convinces employers that the applicant will be an asset.
* How to find job openings before they're advertised.
* How to get 400% more job interviews with a personal letter, resume and phone follow-up technique.
* How to control job interviews by keeping strengths out front—and wind up with a 92% greater chance of being hired!

the allied health series

*All growth begins with
the physical basis of
life—all helping must too.*

Get Fit for Living, Trainer's Guide is a manual for teachers and trainers who wish to increase the energy level of the people they work with. Extensive steps for group diagnosis, training and individual advanced program development are covered. Used together these two books make an ideal trainer-trainee package for complementing helper training programs. 6.95

Get Fit for Living is a handbook for parents, students and trainees who need to learn and act upon the basics of physical functioning: Rest, Diet and Exercises for endurance, strength and flexibility. Personalized diagnosis based on national norms and steps for setting physical goals and implementing the steps toward them are included. 3.95

Members of the health care field like nurses, nurse's aides, doctors, physical therapists and physical trainers need to be able to relate to patients to understand their emotional problems as they cure their medical problems. With timely examples drawn from the files of effective health care workers, this text offers health care personnel the interpersonal expertise they can use to complement their medical technical skills. **The Art of Health Care** teaches interpersonal skills like attending, responding to feelings and their reasons, personalizing and initiating in addition to decision-making and planning skills. 4.95

Helping Begins at Home is a lively and stimulating parenting handbook for people who want to learn how to keep their family together and growing.

Presented within a realistic story are principles and exercises which help parents learn how to build their energy levels, relate better to their children and each other and plan to reach the goals that are important to them. This text can be assigned to parents when you are involving them in the process of helping their children. 3.95

As a helper or trainer in a school or teaching setting, you may often need to involve the child's teacher in your efforts to improve his or her school performance. Published in conjunction with NEA, **Teacher as Person** is a manual for teaching teachers how to respond more fully to their students' emotional worlds. Woven around a captivating allegory of school life are concrete examples of the use and results of attending skills, responding skills, personalizing skills and initiating skills. This is the step you can use to help teachers help you with the child. 3.50

The Promise of America Print 5.00

For those of you who were moved by Dr. Carkhuff's 1974 APGA Keynote Address and wish to share its richness and power with your friends, a limited edition print is now available. Display it proudly wherever people live, learn and work. And remember, this print makes an inspiring gift for friends and loved ones who appreciate and strive to live up to the Promise.

the support series

HRD Press, Box 863, Dept. M-35, Amherst, MA 01002, (413) 253-3489

	Unit Price	Quantity	Price
Trainer Series			
Teaching as Treatment	9.95		
Art of Helping (Trainer's Guide)	9.95		
Art of Developing a Career (Helper's Guide)	9.95		
Trainer Series (above 3)	23.00		
Life Skills Model Videotapes			
Helping Model Module	250.00		
Problem Solving Model Module	250.00		
Program Development Model Module	250.00		
Life Skills Videotape Set (above 3)	635.00		
Art of Helping Training Videotapes			
Attending Skills	200.00		
Responding Skills	200.00		
Personalizing Skills	200.00		
Initiating Skills	200.00		
Art of Helping Training Videotape Set (above 4)	675.00		
Art of Helping Demonstration Videotapes			
The Case of Jerry	250.00		
The Case of Jane	200.00		
The Case of Manny	250.00		
Art of Helping Demonstration Set (above 3)	595.00		
Videotape Sets			
Any two of above sets (25% discount)	1125.00		
All three of above sets (35% discount)	1460.00		
Audio Cassette Tape Packages			
Teacher-Student Tape Package	25.00		
Counselor-Counselee Tape Package	25.00		
Correctional Helper-Inmate Tape Package	25.00		
Human Relations: Racism/Sexism Tape Package	25.00		
All Four Audiotape Packages	75.00		
Perspective Series			
Belly to Belly	6.95		
Cry Twice!	6.95		
Confrontation	6.95		
Perspective Series (above 3)	18.00		
Life Skills Series			
The Art of Helping	5.95		
The Art of Problem Solving	5.95		
How to Help Yourself: The Art of Program Development	5.95		
The Life Skills Series (above 3)	15.00		

	Unit Price	Quantity	Price
Career Skills Series			
The Art of Developing a Career (Student's Guide)	6.95		
GETAJOB	6.95		
Junior High Career Comic	3.95		
Elementary School Career Comic	3.45		
Career Student Sample Kit (above 4)	15.00		
The Allied Health Series			
The Art of Health Care	4.95		
Get Fit for Living	3.95		
Get Fit for Living, Trainer's Guide	6.95		
The Allied Health Series (above 3)	12.00		
The Support Series			
Helping Begins at Home	3.95		
Teacher as Person	3.50		
The Support Series (above 2)	6.00		
The Promise of America Print	5.00		
HRD Catalog Package (everything listed above)	$1495.00		
	Subtotal		
	Postage and Handling .35/book		
	Total		

Name_____ Send order and check to:

Address_____

City_____ State_____ Zip_____

HRD Press
Box 863, Dept. N
Amherst, MA 01█

Telephone_____ Terms: *Payment with order*
    (area code)   *unless accompanied*
                                     by official
                                     purchase order.